Missouri Folklore Society Journal

Special Issue

Folklore and Heritage Studies

Volume 37
2015

Missouri Folklore Society Journal

(Volume 37, 2015)

Special Issue

Folklore and Heritage

edited by

Gregory Hansen & Michelle Stefano

General Editors
Dr. Jim Vandergriff (Ret.)
Dr. Donna Jurich
University of Arizona

Missouri Folklore Society
P. O. Box 1757
Columbia, MO 65205
2019

This issue of the *Missouri Folklore Society Journal* was published by Naciketas Press, 715 E. McPherson, Kirksville, Missouri, 63501

ISSN: 0731-2946; ISBN: 978-1-936135-81-3 (1-936135-81-7)

The *Missouri Folklore Society Journal* is indexed in:

The *Hathi Trust Digital Library*: Vols. 4-24, 26; 1982-2002, 2004. This library essentially acts as an online keyword indexing tool; only allows users to search by keyword and only within one year of the journal at a time. The result is a list of page numbers where the search words appear. No abstracts or full-text incl. (Available free at http://catalog.hathitrust.org/Search/Advanced).

The *MLA International Bibliography*: Vols. 1-26, 1979-2004. Searchable by keyword, author, and journal title. The result is a list of article citations; it does not include abstracts or full-text.

RILM Abstracts of Music Literature: Vols. 13-14, 20; 1991-92, 1998. Searchable by keyword, author, and journal title. Indexes only selected articles about music that appear in these volumes only. Most of the entries have an abstract. There is no full-text.

A list of major articles in every issue of the journal also appears on the Society's web page. Go to *http://missourifolkloresociety.truman.edu/MFS-Jcnts.html*.

Notice to library subscribers and catalogers:
Though the cover date on this volume is 2015, the volume was actually published in 2019.

The Society's board is working to produce enough issues to catch up with the journal's publishing schedule as quickly as possible.

Contents

Gregory Hansen: Connecting Folklore to Heritage Studies

Heritage Studies is a nascent movement that integrates the study of historical and cultural resources into both academic research and applied projects and public programming. Folklorists have contributed to the coalescence of heritage discourse in both implicit and overt ways. Signature contributions include Burt Feintuch's 1988 edited volume *The Conservation of Culture: Folklorists and the Public Sector* and Mary Hufford's 1994 *Conserving Culture: A New Discourse on Heritage*. The idea framing public folklore within the wider rubric of "heritage" has its own legacy that remains vibrant in state and national programming. The inspiration for this current issue of *Missouri Folklore* was sparked by folklorists' engagement in international heritage studies conferences and their contributions to subsequent publications. Within this flourishing heritage discourse, folklorists have worked to discover where we connect with other heritage professionals, and we have also found areas where we can contribute to the conversation. This type of interdisciplinary interest in the heritage movement was clearly evident during the 2016 international conference of the Association for Critical Heritage Studies (ACHS) in Montreal when members of the U. S. Chapter met to discuss future steps. One result was the 2017 meeting, *Connecting (to) Heritage Studies in the U.S.: A Consortium* which was held June 16-18th at Arkansas State University in conjunction with A-State's Heritage Studies Doctoral Program. The focus was to bring scholars and practitioners from a range of disciplines together to find ways to make transdisciplinary connections around approaches for researching, interpreting, and presenting historical and culture resources as heritage. The consortium included short position pieces from scholars and professionals within a variety of disciplines, and the event also included more conventional conference presentations. The goal was to frame out key interests and stimulate discussion. This special issue is designed to represent, in print, some of the key themes and points of discussion from this consortium. The meeting organizers asked presenters and attendees of the event to create written versions of their presentations. To enlarge the scope of discussion, we also enlisted other writers to share their perspectives. The idea is to show points of connection between various interests rather than to provide more conventionally oriented scholarship. In this respect, this issue should be read more as a forum than as an academic tome. Each short position piece is designed to explore heritage studies in relation to a specific discipline or orientation.

Michelle Stefano and I offer these as lightly edited manuscripts that show some key interests from our heritage consortium participants. We include points where writers both agree and disagree; we wanted to illustrate a variety of perspectives within the contemporary heritage discourse. Along with the interdisciplinary scope, we worked to elicit folkloristic angles, and we invite our readers to explore ways that folklorists might further engage with points of similarity and difference between disciplines. Throughout this project, Michelle has focused our attention beyond simply considering heritage studies as a way to connect folklore with related disciplines in applied work. Rather, she has shared her own background to offer fresh perspectives from heritage studies as an academic discipline. In her introduction to critical heritage studies, she challenges us to think beyond the more conventional idea of heritage as a celebration of history and culture. The emergent view of heritage studies calls for more critical perspectives on heritage; writers taking this approach ask us to think of the *heritagization* of historical and cultural resources in terms of process and performance. This contextual approach in heritage studies should be particularly resonant with ways that folklorists conceptualize the traditional expressions that constitute folklife. Her brief overview of critical heritage studies that is included in this volume served as an important presentation at the consortium, and the points that she raised were thoroughly explored throughout the meeting.

The emphasis on creating a printed representation of a wide-ranging and interdisciplinary forum on heritage is only one focus within this special issue. As the project developed, we wanted to insure that enough content within this publication was directly relevant to Missouri. The discussion of ways in which agricultural history and wider social history are interpreted at heritage sites in Arkansas proved especially relevant to heritage studies in the Show-Me state. For example, the activism of the Southern Tenant Farmers' Union, which Ruth Hawkins discusses, crosses state boundaries; areas in the Missouri Bootheel were hotspots for union activity. Hawkins also writes of the development of farmland by Paul Pfieffer, who created a hybrid version of real estate development and tenant farming in the Piggott, Arkansas, area. The Pfieffer family had moved from St. Louis to Piggott in 1913, and their story includes numerous Missouri connections. Ruth, herself, was originally from St. Louis. During the 2017 meeting, the director of the A-State Heritage Studies Doctoral Program, Lauri Umansky, honored Hawkins' with a special event that commemorated her inclusion in the Arkansas Women's Hall of Fame. We honor her achievements in creating Heritage Sites by featuring her article as an example of collaborative work. Her projects involve folklorists, historic preservationist, museum professionals, historians, and students in creating and managing heritage sites.

Monument to union-organized strike of 1939,
US Highway 62, near Charleston, Missouri

Following the consortium, Michelle and I explored how another native Missourian has also made valuable contributions to heritage discourse. As we read through some of Barry Bergey's writings, we discovered his expertise at connecting folklore to heritage studies through his work with the

National Endowment for the Arts and other folklife organizations. Bergey generously provided us with a range of his writings on this topic. We are interspersing his work with various position pieces and photographs in honor of his service to public folklore. In this respect, this volume can be read as a *festschrift*. Barry has recently retired, and Ruth Hawkins has announced her own retirement. Their contributions are clearly part of the *heritagescape* of the region, and their legacy is preserved in tangible sites as well as in their own words.

In reviewing the manuscripts and assembling this volume, it was interesting to discover how heritage studies merges academic research with applied work. Disciplines such as anthropology and sociology have long histories of incorporating applied work into their theory and practice. Other disciplines have a shorter history of ways to engage the public with their subject matter outside of academia. Folklore and ethnomusicology both maintain an interesting history of engaging with non-academic research and public programming. Whereas the idea that there is an overt dichotomy between academic and public folklore is not nearly as contentious as it has been, there remain important differences to consider when we compare "pure" and "applied" research endeavors. The heritage studies movement, however, is built on a foundation of integrating theory and practice. In this respect, those of us engaged in heritage discourse have opportunities to contribute to the dialogue by sharing experiences from applied folklore and ethnomusicology. As the writing within this volume demonstrates, both practitioners and theoreticians are constantly engaging in critical reflection about the dynamics of placing historical and cultural resources into the public sphere. The work of the scholar has obvious contributions for those engaged in public and applied projects. Within heritage studies, another position also emerges. As conscientious and insightful practitioners have demonstrated in their writing, the various ways of putting heritage to use (within museums, festivals, exhibits, historic preservation and other non-academic resources) open up potential new areas of inquiry within academic research. Just as theory must inform practice, the work of practitioners can also inform various approaches, methods, and theories connected to ways that history and culture are represented *as heritage* to a wide range of audiences. This volume is designed to contribute to this most important cultural conversation.

References

Feintuch, Burt (Ed.). (1988). *The Conservation of culture: Folklorists and the public sector.* Lexington: University of Kentucky Press.

"Ruth Hawkins." (2017) Biographical sketch within the Arkansas Women's
     Hall of Fame. http://www.arwomenshalloffame.com/ruth-hawkins/
Hufford, Mary (Ed.). (1994). *Conserving culture: A new discourse on her-
     itage. A Publication of the American Folklore Society.* Urbana and
     Chicago: University of Illinois Press.

Michelle L. Stefano: Connecting to *Critical* Heritage Studies in the U.S.

Founded in 2011, the Association of Critical Heritage Studies (ACHS) serves as a useful organization for opening up dialogue on critical heritage studies and critical heritage work here, in the U.S. Despite the fact that heritage studies – let alone *critical* heritage studies – does not have a longstanding history here (relative to its strong footing elsewhere), this special issue – and the 2017 meeting by which it was inspired – signals that principles and practices from a number of U.S.-based disciplines are already aligned with this emerging, critical movement and, taken together, can contribute greatly to it. Enhancing an exchange of ideas and practice around cultural heritage within the U.S. and with our international peers, through the critical heritage studies scholarship and discourse, was a main impetus for establishing a U.S. chapter of ACHS in early 2013. Moreover, it was the inspiration behind organizing the 2017 *Connecting (to) Heritage Studies in the U.S.* consortium, which was made possible with the generous support of Arkansas State University.

At the moment, ACHS represents an international network of close to 3,000 scholars, professionals, researchers and students, who share a goal of promoting a more critical engagement with 'cultural heritage' in its wide-ranging applications across diverse sociocultural and geographic contexts. At its heart, the association reflects the growing need for a *critical* heritage studies to cast in high relief – and interrogate – the political forces involved with shaping and using cultural heritage, whether tangible, intangible, built and/or natural. In its founding manifesto – or "provocation" – engaging in critical heritage studies is to:

> [C]ritically engage with the proposition that heritage studies

needs to be rebuilt from the ground up, which requires the 'ruthless criticism of everything existing'. Heritage is, as much as anything, a political act and we need to ask serious questions about the power relations that 'heritage' has all too often been invoked to sustain. Nationalism, imperialism, colonialism, cultural elitism, Western triumphalism, social exclusion based on class and ethnicity, and the fetishising of expert knowledge have all exerted strong influences on how heritage is used, defined and managed. (ACHS, 2012)

Conceptualizing cultural heritage as inherently political helps to illuminate historical and contemporary power imbalances that, for instance, work to omit certain histories, stories, and voices from official, dominant, and/or mainstream cultural heritage narratives at global, national, regional, and local levels. For example, what is the official cultural heritage of a nation, and how is it constructed – that is, how and where do we come to learn this official narrative? Most importantly, who is in control of shaping it – whether historically or currently? Then, extend that line of questioning to the regional and local level, to cultural traditions presented on a performance stage, or to one small display case in a museum. In essence, critical heritage studies calls for an examination of who is in control of (and involved with) identifying, designating, interpreting and disseminating heritage, and who is not and, thus, should be.

I always like to use David Lowenthal's definition of cultural heritage, as I first read it in his 1985 book, *The Past is a Foreign Country*. Paraphrasing him, cultural heritage can be considered as a process whereby we collect, utilize, and valorize objects, places, and ideas from the past *in the present* with a view towards preserving them – whether tangible, intangible, or both – for the future. It's a handy notion that helps with differentiating heritage from history. Nonetheless, cultural heritage is very much – if not only – about the present; it reflects the "predilections," biases, and agendas of those who have the power to designate, interpret, and disseminate materials from the past as cultural heritage for today and tomorrow. With this, we can ask: what gets left behind, muted, neglected, and/or purposefully erased? In this respect, heritage can also be seen as a performance. When heritage is placed into the public sphere, the various performances of heritage and its users may not only amplify dominant narratives and further solidify them, but may exclude other configurations of history and culture from what has been termed the 'authorized heritage discourse' (Smith 2006). We can see this performance most recently with the monuments to confederate history and the tensions they create, including the strong desire among many to take them down, off of their literal and proverbial pedestals as official symbols of the cultural heritage of the U.S. South.

As a discipline, heritage studies has always been focused on its public-facing, professional sectors, such as museums and heritage sites, as they are intimately connected to each other. This is to say that heritage studies includes a substantial and equally important applied component: it examines and proposes not only theories relating to cultural heritage and its uses, but the real-world methods, practices, and techniques drawn upon to identify, designate, interpret and disseminate it by professionals and other influential decision-makers across the globe. This deep link to its related professional sector is not unique to heritage studies; public history, historic preservation, applied anthropology, and especially public folklore and applied ethnomusicology, are also concerned with heritage-related practice in the public sphere.

A more critical heritage studies, taking on board the aforementioned questions, proposes ways in which neglected histories, stories, and voices can be amplified, as well as ways to disrupt and *complicate* dominant understandings of and decision-making processes in cultural heritage, to name just one example. Here, the notion of turning critical heritage studies into critical heritage *work* comes to light, and can entail collaborating with communities, groups, and individuals to ensure that they are more involved with (and ideally in control of) representing *themselves* – in their own words and on their own terms – within the heritage enterprise, such as in libraries, archives, museum exhibitions, neighborhood tours, or on those entertaining festival stages.

Viewing critical heritage studies as a discipline that promotes interventions into dominant narratives and ideas, it becomes clear that it overlaps greatly with a wide range of disciplines concerned with the same inquiries and activities here, in the U.S. The kind of critical heritage work promoted by ACHS strongly resonates with the heritage-related initiatives, programs, and projects that are undertaken at the local level across the country and, as evidenced in the articles that follow, particularly in the South. There are plethora of lesser-known, too-long-neglected, cultural heritages of the South that are in need of amplification and dissemination to wider publics, such as the memories and experiences of Japanese-Americans interned during WWII at the Rohwer War Relocation Center, in McGehee, Arkansas, once a relocation camp for thousands and now a museum for all. This heritage was presented by museum staff at the 2017 consortium.

Indeed, the strong focus on local-level efforts in the Arkansas region was one of the key strengths of the 2017 meeting, as well as an important reflection of the aims of critical heritage studies. Managers and staff at regional museums and heritage sites, presented case studies based on their work as professionals on the 'front lines' of heritage practice, foregrounding organizational missions and strengths, as well as the challenges that they face. Participants traveled from all over the U.S. (and beyond) to the consortium, which emerged as an opportunity to engage in these on-the-ground 'reality checks,' and to exchange ideas on effective ways forward. Discussions underscored that many obstacles in doing critical heritage work are commonly confronted across diverse contexts and, as such, more conversations such as these need to be encouraged.

Another strength of the consortium was its interdisciplinarity, which was intentionally fostered during the planning stages and, in turn, is certainly reflected in this special issue. The articles draw on the knowledges and reflections of scholars and professionals situated in an array of disciplines and sectors – from heritage management, folklore and public folklore to historic preservation and cultural conservation. In this light, critical heritage studies can be viewed as a tool for bringing together different, yet overlapping, perspectives on both theory and practice, opening up space for dialogue and action. From the perspective of ACHS, increasing interdisciplinarity in heritage studies is an integral requirement for ensuring its criticality.

Among eight specific actions, including the establishment of a global network (i.e. ACHS), scholars and practitioners alike are asked in the manifesto to: draw upon wider intellectual sources, such as those represented here, to "provide theoretical insights and techniques to study 'heritage;'" collect 'data' that "challenge the established conventions of positivism and quantitative analysis" from a broader range of sources in "novel and imaginative ways"; democratize heritage by "consciously rejecting elite cultural narratives" and, as mentioned earlier, embrace the "heritage insights" of communities, groups and individuals who have traditionally been excluded in the preservationist paradigm, particularly with respect to recognizing 'non-Western' cultural heritage traditions; and promote "debate between researchers, practitioners and communities" (ACHS, 2012). Interspersed throughout this issue are the contributions of Barry Bergey, the Director of the Folk and Traditional Arts program at the National Endowment for the Arts (2000-2014). Bergey's pieces provide excellent examples of the types of interdisiciplinary overlaps regarding cultural equity, identity, sustainability, and ever-changing cultural expressions which can further democratize heritage, heritage practice, and related discourse.

With this in mind, the issue – taken as a whole – prompts important questions that can be asked within the context of U.S.-based heritage practice. In particular: can we use the critical heritage studies movement to connect more to each other? From our wide-ranging theoretical bases and with our different methodological toolkits, we are commonly concerned with the power relations that shape the historical and sociocultural phenomena we study. Often, we are concerned with our professional conduct, which we strive to make more just and ethical. Yet, are there divides between us, in terms of disciplinary borders, that ought to be broken down? And how can that happen? As there is a very active international heritage discourse, I say, let us connect more to it and expand it.

References

ACHS. (2012). "2012 Manifesto." Available at: https://www.criticalheritagestudies.org/history/ (accessed 26 January 2019).

Lowenthal, David (1985). *The Past is a foreign country*. Cambridge: Cambridge University Press.

Smith, Laurajane (2006). *The Uses of heritage*. London and New York: Routledge.

Short Biography of Barry Bergey

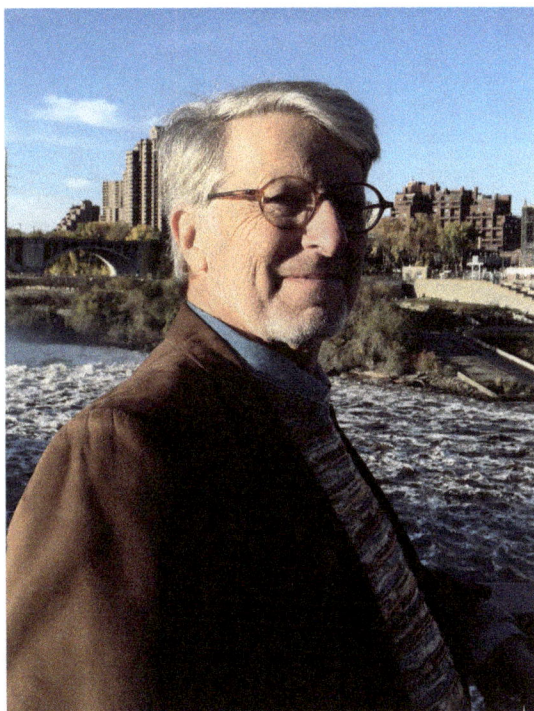

Barry Bergey grew up in New Haven, Missouri, and studied American Literature at the University of Missouri - Columbia (B.A., 1966) and Washington University in St. Louis (M.A., 1968). He co-founded the Missouri Friends of the Folk Arts, a non-profit organization dedicated to the documentation and presentation of traditional artists. As its Director, he

1

co-produced recordings (*I'm Old But I'm Awfully Tough: Traditional Music of the Ozark Region*), radio programs (The Missouri Tradition), and festivals (the Frontier Folklife Festival held on the grounds of the Gateway Arch). After serving as the first state folk arts coordinator for the State of Missouri for three years, in 1985 he took a position as Folk Arts Specialist at the National Endowment for the Arts. In 2000 he became director of that program and held that position until his retirement in 2014. During his tenure at the NEA, he worked with the U.S. Department of State, UNESCO, and the World Bank on policies related to intangible cultural heritage. This past year he collaborated with photographer Tom Pich on the book *Folk Masters: A Portrait of America* published by Indiana University Press.

Barry Bergey: Folk & Traditional Arts: Challenges And Opportunities

[This report was written by Barry Bergey, on March 1, 2010.]

Background

The folk and traditional arts encompass multiple artistic genres that are often characterized by specific and well-defined aesthetic conventions. While frequently shaped by unique geographic settings and maintained by distinct cultural communities, the folk arts are widely practiced and broadly dispersed. The knowledge and skills of folk artists are usually passed along in informal settings and customarily are taught through rigorous one-on-one apprenticeships. Folk arts are rooted in heritage but are in a constant state of evolution and are responsive to contemporary cultural circumstance.

Folk and traditional arts might be viewed from three perspectives:

1. An artistic genre – Folk & traditional arts could be considered to be an array of artistic genres, including music, crafts, dance, storytelling, and other creative expressions, learned as part of the cultural life of a community whose members often share a common ethnic heritage, language, religion, occupation, or geographic region. These traditions are shaped by the aesthetics and values of a shared culture and are passed from generation to generation, most often within family

3

and community through observation, conversation, and practice. If understood as personal expression in the context of community, folk and traditional arts can also be viewed as organic and dynamic, responding to ever-changing aesthetic values and civic circumstances.

2. A field – Folk & traditional arts could be considered to be a field characterized as a culturally diverse and geographically dispersed collection of public and private organizations. For the most part, these nonprofit organizations are small and many are culturally specific. A survey of self-identified folk arts institutions in the mid-90's revealed that of over 400 organizations, 72% had annual budgets of under $150,000. Complementing the work of the nonprofit organizations is a network of statewide and regional folk arts programs, most of which are based at state arts agencies, regional arts organizations, or other public institutions. The field has no official membership-based service organization, although organizations such as the National Council for the Traditional Arts, American Folklore Society, and National Network for Folk Arts in Education do have a national purview. At the federal level, in addition to the NEA, institutions such as the American Folklife Center at the Library of Congress, the Center for Folklife and Cultural Heritage at the Smithsonian Institution, the National Endowment for the Humanities, and the Institute for Museums and Library Services, are engaged with folk cultural funding and/or programming.

3. A realm of expertise and a cultural strategy – Most specialists in the field of folk and traditional arts have training in folklore, ethnomusicology, cultural anthropology, American studies, or related areas of cultural study. Several principles and strategies have been key to the work of the field: a) discovery – the need to continually do fieldwork to identify and document artists and communities, especially given our mobile and newcomer populations; b) context – the responsibility to recognize and present artists and art forms with an understanding of their social, cultural and historical background; c) education – the importance of apprenticeships, workshops, residencies, curriculum-based arts learning, and well-interpreted public programs in conserving cultural traditions; d) diversity – the importance of understanding and appreciating multiple aesthetic traditions and standards of excellence when working with folk artists and culturally distinct communities.

Cultural Conversation

A recent weeklong blog discussion on *Arts Journal* devoted considerable screen space to the question "Expressive life: Do we need a new framework for culture?" The supposition was that terms such as art and culture had outlived their usefulness and that expressive life might be a better way to frame a conversation about cultural policy in the 21st century. The two elements of the expressive continuum, the north and south magnetic poles, were defined as heritage - tradition, community, shared values, historical practices – and voice – autonomy, distinctiveness, personality, and innovation. The hope, as conveyed by many of the discussants, was that this new nomenclature might both broaden the cultural policy playing field and focus the mission of advocates for arts and culture. These sorts of discussions are not new to the field of folklore, as scholars and public activists have long debated the heavily freighted terminology associated with words such as "folk," "authentic," "lore," and "primitive," to name just a few. During this discussion, I will use some of these terms interchangeably and sometimes, I might shorten our programmatic title to folk arts for the sake of space, with the understanding that in broader policy terms we're still dealing with an imperfect semantic universe.

To revisit the magnetic metaphor, the folk arts often function at latitudes between the two poles of heritage and voice, where the attraction of both tradition and innovation are at play. NEA National Heritage Fellow Irvin Trujillo, a seventh generation weaver from northern New Mexico who first pursued a career as a civil engineer, designs and weaves rugs in the Chimayo tradition. Each woven piece is one-of-a-kind and strikingly innovative, but when he speaks of his work he says: "I am trying to approach the spirit of the old pieces. In doing that, I need to learn from the past, but [also] how to live in my time and environment." One of his rugs portrays a human figure with a long shadow stretching across the pattern of the weaving. The figure is silhouetted, so it is impossible to tell which way the person is facing; so, as Irvin tells it, this piece might be about the past, or the future, or both. For folk artists and specialists who work in the field, conversation between past and present, tradition and innovation, the community and the individual is ongoing.

Who Owns Culture?

When Russian ice dancers Oksana Domnina and Maxim Shabalin took the ice at the Vancouver Olympic Competition in costumes inspired by Australian aboriginal body décor and design and performed their program to music that incorporated the didgeridoo, a traditional instrument, there was an outcry from aboriginal leaders that this constituted cultural theft. One Councilwoman from the Australian state of New South Wales said: "Our dance, our ceremony and even how we look is the basis of much of our culture. Our designs and images have evolved over 60,000 years.... For many of us, our culture is all we have left." But, who owns culture? Can a group restrict access to their artistic achievements, when copyright laws have historically protected only individual and corporate ownership? Was there the same sense of outrage when in the same competition a German pair did a Hawaiian dance, a Chinese pair did a Greek dance, a British pair did an American dance, and an American pair did an Asian Indian dance? The question of who owns and who controls the use of artistic work and cultural heritage will be, I feel, central to our cultural conversation in the coming decades.

In a recent article in *The New Republic* Lawrence Lessig points out that copyright issues now touch almost everyone and everything in our lives. With the rise of digital reproduction, distribution, and reconfiguration, the concept of fair use is more and more making access to our culture a legally regulated event that he characterizes as a "catastrophic cultural mistake." Lessig argues that restrictions on copying threaten our ability to preserve documentary film and old recordings. He concludes:

> I only know that the two extremes that are before us would, each of them, if operating alone, be awful for our culture. The one extreme, pushed by copyright abolitionists, that forces free access on every form of culture, would shrink the range and diversity of culture. I am against abolitionism. And I see no reason to support the other extreme either – pushed by the content industry – that seeks to license every single use of culture, in whatever context. That extreme would radically shrink access to our past.

Folklorists and cultural specialists have the opportunity to play a central role in these cultural conversations about ownership and access. For the past several years the World Intellectual Property Organization (WIPO) has been convening a working group tasked with making recommendations on the subject of "Traditional Knowledge, Genetic Resources and Folklore/Traditional Cultural Expressions." It remains to be seen if a legal regime of protection and regulation will result. Most of the practical applications of principles related to ownership and access will depend on the knowledge, skills, and sensitivities of those who document and present the creative work of cultural communities. Anthropologist Michael F. Brown sums this up in his book *Who Owns Native Culture?*:

I am so impressed by the hope and pragmatism of indigenous elders, museum curators, archivists, and cultural-resource managers who are negotiating their way to more balanced relationships. They, far more than the activists and academic theorists who set the terms of debate about cultural ownership, understand that progress will be built on small victories, innovative local solutions, and frequent compromise. They recognize, too, that a world ruled solely by proprietary passions is not a world in which most of us want to live.

The Human Touch

Lance Lee, an astute folk arts panelist with experience as the founder of an apprenticeship program in wooden boat building, often pointed to the high tech versus high touch dichotomy in discussing folk arts applications. High touch is metaphorically conflated with concepts of authenticity and traditionality, but today these choices are not always so clear. Master instrument builder and National Heritage Fellow Wayne Henderson uses both a pocket knife and an electric belt sander to make his handcrafted guitars, while the microphone, the mixing board, and the sound monitor are as important to bluegrass musicians as the acoustic instruments themselves. In more extreme examples, how will long-arm electric sewing machines change quilting traditions? Will the community quilting circle be replaced by individual studio-based quilt production? Will AutoTune electronics and digital sampling re-define what we understand as folk music? On a front more familiar to the general public, the commercial movie world is debating whether live "performance capture" actors in such computer-generated animation films such as *Avatar* should be honored with Oscars.

When the only constant is change, concepts of authenticity and tradition are evolving and dynamic constructs. The most recent issue of *Paste* magazine uses the bold red and black graphics of the 1966 "Is God Dead?" issue of *Time* to ask "Is Indie Dead?" The author proclaims that the fan base for this counter-cultural music, also known through the years as "punk," or "alternative," has held to their own version of anti-mainstream authenticity. As these musical forms have connected more and more with cultural commodities through their use in advertising and in gaming and television sound tracks, the music, by whatever name, has lost its oppositional cachet. The writer asks: "So what do we do now that the one common factor in anyone's definition of 'indie,' the one thing about indie we thought we could rely on – its authenticity, its unsullied artistry – has been indicted?"

Each artistic movement and each artistic genre seems to work out its own metrics for authenticity. With access to information and to cultural commodities easier and faster than ever, and our choices almost limitless, the filtering process is still an important one. The algorithms of excellence are still a challenge. Web sites such as *etsy* open up convenient markets for individual craftspeople, but a curatorial or educational dimension is often lost in the process. Time and dime seem to trump quality and curation as gatekeepers for the vast array of products available on the site. Will iTunes and YouTube become increasingly difficult to navigate without increasingly sophisticated wayfinders?

In making qualitative judgments in the funding process at a federal agency we wrestle with these issues. The panel process returns us to the primacy of the human touch. Decisions are only as good as our panels, for panelists are able to bring to the process the various dimensions of quality, including the "text, context, and texture" of the work before them. This provides what anthropologist Mary Catherine Bates calls the peripheral vision necessary to make informed decisions about our cultural priorities.

The Virtue Of Place Meets Virtual Space

In the early 1970s NEA senior staff took a trip to southwestern Louisiana to visit master Cajun fiddler Dewey Balfa, later to be named a National Heritage Fellow. Here is Dewey's account of the visit:

> Our good friend Alan Jabbour, who was with the National Endowment then, asked if it was possible for some of the people to come down to see this part of the country. He arranged for me to make a gumbo. I can remember some of the officers.... I didn't know who I was talking to, but we got into a discussion about the regions.... I can remember telling the chairman afterwards, 'If I was to go in your part of the country and you were going to feed me gumbo and sauce piquant, why I'd just as well stay down here.' I said, 'If I had the same culture you had, and vice versa, chances are you'd have never come down here.'

Or, as Alan Lomax succinctly put it when speaking about the tendency toward what he called cultural grey-out, the polluting sameness of popular culture: "pretty soon there will be no place on the earth worth visiting – and no particular reason to stay home either."

So, the question might have become: do we any longer have reason to venture outside our homes, let alone visit another cultural or natural environment? The folk arts field has generally celebrated the expression of a sense of place, the unique aesthetic qualities and traditions of particular communities and regions. What is the place for regionally distinct and community-based arts in virtual space? Jason Lanier, a computer scientist who popularized the term "virtual reality" has recently published a more sobering look at the new technological landscape entitled *You Are Not a Gadget*. He warns that "When technologies deploy a computer model of something like learning or friendship in a way that has an effect on real lives, they are relying on faith. When they ask people to live their lives through their models, they are potentially reducing life itself." In his own description of cultural grey-out and its impact on the arts, Michael Antman in a feature on the website *Pop Matters* entitled "The Future is an Empty Room" says: "The effect of digital technologies (and here I'm not referring solely to the Internet) on the quality of our arts has been disastrous, blenderizing and pureeing the original, the authentic, and the indigenous into a kind of flavorless digital slurry." Anyone for gumbo and sauce piquant?

While a Nielsen-funded report from the Center for Research Excellence indicates that we now spend between 8 ½ and 9 ½ hours a day looking at a screen; a recent *Washington Post* article points out that young people are on average delaying getting their driver's licenses at the age of 16 because they no longer need vehicles to communicate with their friends. The down side is that it appears to reaffirm the trope that we are becoming a nation of digital shut-ins. The up side is that these new means of communication might make it possible for people to stay in a desired place to get a job and thus reinforce commitment to family, to home community, and to geographic distinctiveness.

Digital technologies also offer exciting means of preservation and distribution of content. In the field of folk arts, we are content-rich and institution-poor, so the use of digital media to make materials accessible may well allow low cost and labor efficient ways to reach new audiences. Websites such as Folkstreams, American Memory: Online Collections of the American Folklife Center at the Library of Congress, and Global Sound on Smithsonian Folkways, all allow access to important archival materials of documentary film and recorded sound from around the world. Documentation conducted by state and regional folk arts programs across the country are being digitized and put on the web. Many states also are developing web-based educational materials geared toward folk arts in education programs. Still, the digital revolution has not reached all quarters – a recent Country Music Association poll revealed that only half of country music consumers have home Internet connection.

Digital innovation has fostered the DIY (Do it yourself) revolution. More and more musicians and documentary filmmakers are bypassing the standard systems of production and distribution of their work. While there has been a worrying trend toward the consolidation of major media gate-keepers, individual artists are using readily available digital equipment to produce their own work, and they use social networking media to reach new audiences. Geoff Boucher, writing in the *Los Angeles Times*, says: "YouTube, Facebook, Twitter and MySpace are the places where bands lay circuitry for success these days." He quotes Steven Scott, a guitarist and singer with a band called the Afternoons: "Art, fashion, live performance are the things that help us connect now. We think if people hear the music and what we have to say, then we can start a relationship with them."

Maybe it's all about relationships after all. Michael Wolff writes in *Vanity Fair* – "The Internet, with a flat hierarchy, cheap distribution, and virtually no production barriers, lets people express themselves more naturally. We're collaborative animals, it turns out, and joyful amateurs, interested more in entertaining and informing ourselves than in being entertained and informed by professionals." We have met the artists and they are us. Folklore, defined by some as informal artistic communication in small groups, as a field and as a realm of expertise and cultural strategy, will continue to engage with this organic and ever-changing dynamic of artistic expression and its connection to community, virtual or otherwise. Just as folklorists were in the forefront in recognizing and documenting emergent artistic traditions such as hip hop, graffiti art, body adornment, urban legends, and Xerox lore, public folk arts specialists will continue to engage in identifying and understanding forms of expressive life that result from new technologies and new ways of creating and defining community. However, as Wynton Marsalis reminded us in his 2009 Nancy Hanks lecture, "The technology of the human soul has not changed."

We Are The World! Er, Are We The World?

The opening ceremonies of the Vancouver Olympic Games illustrate another issue facing us in the coming decades – the competing interests of national/international identity. As with the Beijing summer games, the opening celebration allows a nation an opportunity to present itself and its unique character to the rest of the world. Most frequently organizers put their indigenous and time-tested cultural heritage on display. First Nations dancers, drummers, and orators, as well as Francophone Quebecois and Maritime Celtic musicians, were the centerpiece of Canada's self-presentation to the world. How does this connect with a world that in other ways is becoming flatter and flatter? Bau Graves in his book *Cultural Democracy* addresses this question, asserting that:

> Culture is now on the international agenda in a way that it has never been in the past. It is simultaneously a primary point of dispute in the emergent debates over globalization and a primary determinant to how the debate is conducted and perceived within diverse communities worldwide. Further, the outcomes of contemporary policy debates, as they are enacted and become history, will have fundamental implications for how local, regional, national, and global cultures shape themselves and our future. How globalization addresses or suppresses the facts of cultural diversity – and how every local culture contends with globalization – will be the subtext, if not the main story, of the twenty-first century.

In the past, folk and traditional artists have been integral both to nationalism, a nation's unified public and political identity, and to internationalism, a nation's understanding of itself as a culturally diverse and ever-changing population with personal and political global connections. In response to a rising call for cross cultural understanding and public diplomacy, cultural heritage will again, I believe, be central to U.S. foreign policy conversations. The John Brademas Center for the Study of Congress has recently issued a report to the President and Congress entitled "Moving Forward: A Renewed Role for American Arts and Artists in the Global Age." Among recommendations are 1) that international arts and cultural exchanges be integrated into strategies of U.S. policymakers as a key element of public diplomacy; 2) that advanced electronic social networking be utilized in cultural diplomacy; and 3) that a national conversation on the arts generally and their centrality to the quality of American life both home and abroad begin. Clearly, engaging artists that represent the depth and diversity of our cultural heritage would be central to meeting these goals.

Now What?!

The Folk & Traditional Arts program at the NEA has played a leadership role in both developing and maintaining flexible, proactive, and multi-faceted strategies for support of folk and traditional artists and organizations. Critical to this success has been the establishment of a network of cultural specialists around the country to serve as a link with artists and communities. This infrastructure, complementing the NEA's broader strategy of partnership with state, regional, and local arts agencies, provides a limber and responsive framework for connecting with and serving artists and audiences across the nation. Folk arts specialists frequently combine roles as grants administrators, fieldworkers, public programmers, and educators. Embedding folk arts expertise in arts agencies has resulted in a high level of community engagement in our field and has leveraged significant dollars at the state, regional, and local level.

Early infrastructural support has also resulted in the establishment of a number of nonprofit organizations serving local, regional, and national constituencies. While folk arts has a rather light institutional footprint – by most standards our organizations are small to medium sized at best – these organizations are responsive to the needs of their communities and often provide innovative programming that is not possible at the federal or state level. Ongoing funding for folk and traditional arts projects through the Access to Artistic Excellence constitutes the largest proportion of NEA investment in activities of the field. This project-based funding supports public programs such as festivals, concert series, national and regional touring, exhibitions, and media presentations. In addition, support is provided for fieldwork, documentation, and discovery research that leads ultimately to public programs. Grants in Arts Education also support school-based and community-based projects in folk and traditional arts. As noted in a recent discussion with folk arts panelists, Access to Artistic Excellence funding serves both as the stimulus and often the lifeblood, of folk arts active organizations.

In some ways, the establishment of the National Heritage Fellowship program has had the broadest national and even international impact on the public understanding and appreciation of folk and traditional arts. Since 1982 the agency has given the highest form of federal recognition, not to mention much-needed money, to more than 350 artists who represent the excellence and diversity of our cultural heritage.

The agency's leadership role in one area has been lost over the last few years. Previously, through a program called Traditional Arts Growth (TAG), we were able to provide our field technical assistance, program evaluation, professional development, and opportunities for convening. This program allowed the NEA to serve as a leader in the field and a quick responder to smaller not-for-profits, culturally-specific organizations, tribes, and other organizations that might have an immediate need for consultation or assistance. With no official service organization for our field, this allowed the agency to aid in the convening of meetings on field-wide issues, as well as to underwrite travel costs so that folk arts specialists might be at the table in meetings where they often were not able to be present.

Opportunities For The Future: Discovery, Democracy, Development, and Diplomacy

Cultural Discovery

With folk arts specialists situated in state and local arts agencies, as well as nonprofits collaborating with arts agencies, the work of the field has a civic dimension that usually combines administrative, curatorial, and documentary roles. Discovery of new communities, new artistic traditions, and emergent forms of artistic expression is central to the role of folk arts specialists. This approach is especially effective with changing demographics in the United States — including arrival of new immigrant and refugee populations — and with evolving forms of artistic expression which result from advanced technologies and innovative ways of constructing community identity.

A recent study commissioned by the James Irvine Foundation entitled "Cultural Engagement in California's Inland Regions" used techniques of discovery based not on passive assessments, but rather on door-to-door and proactive census techniques, akin to methods used by folklorists. The conclusion was: "Results paint a detailed picture of the breadth and depth of cultural engagement in the two regions and reveal a rich tapestry of activity in music, theatre and drama, reading and writing, dance, and visual arts and crafts – much of which occurs 'off the radar map' of the traditional nonprofit infrastructure of arts organizations and facilities." I believe that the NEA-supported network of folk arts specialists can make a significant contribution to ongoing cultural conversations at the federal level as we explore innovative methodologies for reaching new constituencies.

Cultural Democracy

Cultural democracy is in some ways linked to cultural discovery. Recognizing and respecting the various cultural and aesthetic traditions is central to the projects and programs of folk arts. The National Heritage Fellowships program provides a vivid picture of the artistic diversity of the nation. Other funded programs work across age, class, and cultural distinctions. With their emphasis on family and community, folk arts activities frequently reach multi-cultural and multi-generational audiences through free festivals and concerts. Apprenticeship programs and after-school workshops often allow master artists to work with younger students. Bau Graves speaks of a new paradigm "… a system of support for the cultures of our diverse communities that is respectful and celebratory, that gives voice to the many who have been historically excluded from the public domain, and that makes no claims of superiority or special status. It assumes a fundamental acceptance of difference." Honoring and respecting both excellence and cultural diversity through such programs as the Heritage Fellowships provides a vivid picture of cultural and aesthetic democracy.

Cultural Development

Wendell Berry, writing in *Sex, Economy, Freedom, and Community* says "In order to survive, a plurality of true communities would require not egalitarianism and tolerance but knowledge, an understanding of the necessity of local differences, and respect. Respect, I think, always implies imagination – the ability to see one another, across our inevitable differences, as living souls." Working with local knowledge in the context of a sense of community often provides the platform for cultural development.

This base of knowledge and experience ties in nicely with the "Our Town" concept. Community-wide, as well as culturally-specific, festivals have been a venue for presenting local artists and celebrating local culture for over a century. Preliminary data from our report on outdoor festivals reveals that 43% of the festivals reported folk and traditional arts content, while visual arts/crafts are featured in 67% of the events. Of music festivals, the largest percentage, 53% report that they present folk music. Successful festivals also have the potential to be strong economic drivers – the 2009 National Folk Festival held in Butte, Montana, reports a $17.5 million dollar benefit to the local economy based on a $1.2 million dollar cost.

Within the agency we have discussed the challenges in identifying ways that the "Our Town" model might engage rural and underserved areas. In effect, how does "Our Town" also become "Our Pueblo," "Our Village," "Our Neighborhood," or "Our River Valley?" Heritage tourism initiatives offer opportunities for community building from both an economic and cultural perspective. Recently funded projects addressing heritage tourism, including the Crooked Road Trail in Virginia; the Blue Ridge Music, Craft Heritage, and Cherokee Trails in North Carolina; the New Mexico Fiber Arts Trails; and the Kentucky Quilt Trails have proven to be effective ways to both showcase local culture and to provide economic benefits for folk and traditional artists.

Cultural Diplomacy

Cultural heritage and multiculturalism have become prominent features on the agendas of international and inter-governmental organizations. Within the past five years UNESCO has ratified two conventions (treaties) related to cultural heritage – the Convention for the Safeguarding of the Intangible Cultural Heritage and the Convention on the Protection and Promotion of the Diversity of Cultural Expressions. Although at this point the U.S. has not ratified either convention, NEA staff were involved in the drafting meetings of both of these documents and we continue to consult with the Department of State on these issues. In the international arena the funding strategies and framework of governance related to arts and culture is of great interest to other countries. For many countries, the concept of addressing cultural heritage through programs, rather than centralized regulation or policy, is both new and of interest.

The NEA Heritage Fellowship program has served as a model for other countries as they seek to address intangible cultural heritage. In April an exhibition and series of programs prominently featuring the Heritage Fellowships will be mounted at the UNESCO headquarters during their Executive Board meeting. This will be followed by a publication and a series of exhibitions and programs in five locations in Belgium in July of 2010, highlighting the Heritage Fellows and focusing on ways that non-governmental organizations can address intangible cultural heritage. If the United States does in the future ratify the UNESCO Convention on Intangible Cultural Heritage, it would appear that the NEA could play an even more significant role in meeting the terms of the convention, especially in areas relating to the creation of inventories of intangible cultural heritage and the identification and safeguarding of endangered cultural traditions.

One of the policy planks of the new administration was the enhancement of cultural exchange with other countries. This provides the opportunity for the State Department to again tour artists who accurately reflect the diversity and excellence of American folk and traditional artists. Recognizing that this requires a reciprocal strategy, the arts platform also calls for more open Immigration and Naturalization Service (INS) policies for artists who wish to tour in this country. Again, these are important opportunities for the NEA and Folk & Traditional Arts to contribute to the cultural conversation.

Conclusion

In a report to the National Council on the Arts in 1979, her first describing the newly established Folk Arts Program at the agency, Bess Lomax Hawes said the following:

> In many ways, Folk Arts is in a fortunate position – our handicaps can at times be transformed into advantages. With a potential constituency bordering on the infinite, we can afford to be highly selective (and generally, therefore, pretty successful) in the projects we actually fund. With a limited budget, we can avoid locking ourselves into the annual funding expectations that so often hamstring the larger programs. With the absence of major support organizations, we can stress innovative and imaginative projects, rather than ongoing institutional support.

These words apply for the most part today. Folk and traditional arts as a field remains woefully under-institutionalized, but it seeks to serve a constituency large in number and broad in scope, while remaining responsive to an ever-changing cultural environment. Living up to these challenges will be our continuing goal.

Michael Ann Williams: Heritage and Folklore

During the past half century, the American field of folklore has both expanded its scope and critically deconstructed its fundamental premises. The expansion came both in the form of embracing new genres of study (especially in the areas of belief and material culture), as well as in employment opportunities outside of academia. The concept of heritage has played a significant role in the expansion of applied folklore (both in the growth of public folklore, but also in folklorists' participation in museum work and historic preservation); however, heritage has surprisingly eluded the definitional scrutiny of the era.

During the 1970s, the scholars of the new folkloristics demoted the concept of tradition as central to definitions of folklore, or chose to redefine the notion as an active process of construction. Heritage, tradition's not-quite-identical twin concept, was never quite wrestled to the ground in the same manner as other key words of our discipline. The influential 2003 *Eight Words for the Study of Expressive Culture* (a revised version of an earlier special issue of the *Journal of American Folklore*) examined the definition of tradition, along with art, text, identity, context, genre, performance and group.

Heritage, at times, has served as a cloak, rather than as a key concept, especially for some in the public sector. Those squeamish about use of the term "folk" or who felt the terms "folk" and "tradition" were too limiting, became self-styled "heritage workers." Heritage also provided an umbrella term for folklorists increasingly working within the realms of museums and historic preservation. (My first employment as a public folklorist was at a "Heritage Center"). The label of heritage also found growing currency in governmental agencies. The ill-fated Heritage Conservation Recreation Service (HCRS), formed during the Carter administration and abolished by Reagan's, attempted to unify the management of natural and culture re-

17

sources. In 1980, an amendment to the National Historic Preservation Act called for a report on "preserving and conserving the intangible elements of our cultural heritage." The resulting report conducted by the American Folklife Center at the Library of Congress failed to usefully suggest ways to integrate the preservation of cultural intangibles into the existing preservation law, but it did contribute the useful concept of "cultural conservation" to the dialog.

Throughout the 1980s, the American Folklife Center conducted various pilot projects that unified public folklore with other forms of heritage management. The culmination of their cultural conservation work came with the 1990 conference at the Library of Congress, papers from which were published in *Conserving Culture: A New Discourse on Heritage* (1994) edited by Mary Hufford. Although use of the term "cultural conservation" subsequently waned and the promise of a more unified approach to heritage management has yet to be achieved, the conference and book were a landmark in bringing public folklorists in dialog with others in heritage fields.

The 1980s also brought a growing awareness among American folklorists of heritage regimes in other countries. The establishment of the National Heritage Fellowship program at the National Endowment for the Arts in 1982 was based, in part, on intangible cultural heritage programs in other countries, most notably Japan. The program selects individuals to honor for contributions to "our nation's traditional arts heritage." Similar to the Cultural Conservation report, the program avoids the label "intangible heritage" (despite the inspiration for the program) and prominently uses the word "heritage" rather than "folk."

While heritage has not received the widespread definitional scrutiny of "folk," "tradition," or "genre," modes of heritage production have received considerable scholarly scrutiny from American folklorists in the past twenty years. Among the earliest, and most influential, studies, Barbara Kirshenblatt-Gimblett's examination of the relationship of heritage to museums and tourism in *Destination Culture* (1998) argues that heritage is a mode of production that gives endangered culture a second life as an exhibition of itself and that the possession of heritage is itself a mark of modernity. In 2004, Kirshenblatt-Gimblett examined more specifically UNESCO's role in international intangible cultural heritage safeguarding in her article, "Intangible Heritage as Metacultural Production."

In the past two decades, most of the critical scholarship produced by American folklorists on heritage production has focused on international efforts, especially the UNESCO ICH convention (despite the fact America does not participate in this activity). Perhaps, to a degree, this has been a result on an effort to keep the peace within the domestic home front of our field. Scholars may write critically of heritage protocols without seemingly criticizing friends and colleagues within the American Folklore Society. However, even as deep divisions between academic and public folklore seem to be healing (especially as more and more academic programs jump on the bandwagon of training public folklorists), the arguments on heritage seem to politely ignore some fundamental divides. The logical conclusion from at least some critiques of heritage production would be to look at all publicly funded support of the traditional arts with a jaundiced eye. American folklorists in general have yet to reconcile advocacy for public funding of the traditional arts with suspicion over governmental intervention is heritage activities.

Heritage as a concept needs a more nuanced critique by American folklorists. Scrutiny of international protocols occasionally seem knee jerk in nature. While the act of listing will always be problematic, we need more layered and complex understandings of how governmental support has shaped the public valuation of intangible culture. Governmental interest and funding are not inherently good or evil. We need richer and more complex case studies and it is time to turn our focus to domestic programs again. At the same time, American folklorists should stop using the label "heritage" as an easy substitute for "folklore" or "tradition." Much like the convenient word "vernacular," heritage needs its own definitional scrutiny. It is no less, or more, baggage-free than the other terms we have ruminated on for decades now.

No one who lives in the American South can continue to believe that "heritage" is unproblematic. "Heritage not hate" argued that the embrace of the memorials to and flags of the Confederacy had nothing to do with racism. As one acquaintance of mine who worked professionally in the Civil War heritage profession confided, Charlottesville, Virginia, 2017 was his "Kent State moment." Just as the shooting of unarmed college students in 1970 marked a turning point in the public's feelings about the Vietnam War, the demonstrations and death in Charlottesville makes it all too clear that "heritage" is not an unloaded concept.

References

Feintuch, Burt (Ed.). (2003). *Eight words for the study of expressive culture: Group, art, text, genre, performance, context, tradition, identity*. Urbana/Champaign: University of Illinois Press.

Hufford, Mary (Ed.). (1994). *Conserving culture: A new discourse on heritage*. A Publication of the American Folklore Society, Urbana and Chicago: University of Illinois Press.

Kirshenblatt-Gimblett, Barbara. (1998). *Destination culture: Tourism, museum, and heritage.* Berkeley: University of California Press.

Amanda Minks: Heritage Studies and Indigenous Property: Transforming Law and Policy through Music

Critical Heritage Studies have given us valuable tools to think about people's uses of the past and the instrumentalization of culture. There are some common threads pointing to heightened anxieties about the rapid changes—technological, environmental, cultural—that prompt so many groups of people to focus on heritage. In addition to the sweeping theoretical surveys and collections of diverse case studies, we should also pay attention to the specificity of particular cultural positions and practices. Indigenous cultures have played an important role in the development of international discourses of heritage during the 20th century, but their unique legal status is not always recognized. In the U.S., federally recognized tribes are sovereign entities that maintain a government-to-government relation with the U.S. federal government. Many other countries' legal systems accord special rights to Indigenous peoples, as do the 148 states that approved the UN Declaration on the Rights of Indigenous Peoples.

What about the specificity of music in heritage discourse? Music has often been objectified as heritage through the medium of recordings. Most recordings held in archives were made by non-Indigenous researchers or collectors, under conditions of extreme inequality that did not respect cultural protocols or private, sacred repertoires. Like physical objects such as a piece of pottery, Indigenous music was taken from its communities and placed in institutions for the purpose of non-Indigenous science, aiming to preserve the relics of cultures assumed to be vanishing. But unlike pottery, the embodied, performative qualities of music led to an object — a recording — entering museums and archives as a *copy* rather than as an original. In that copy, a living voice was transformed and displaced away from the person who sang the song. Music is much more mobile than physical objects, especially when it is made available in digital form. Digitized music proliferates and moves in many directions, often escaping the control of those who claim it as heritage or property. In the dominant legal system, the reproduction and circulation of sound recordings are governed by copyright. Copyrights to field recordings are usually held by the person who made the recording, or by a record company or archive if the collector transferred the rights through a donation or sale of the recordings. Copyright is part of an intellectual property regime that has privileged written authors over oral, and individuals over collectives. It is designed to protect economic rights but not cultural rights. While Indigenous groups often seek to limit access to their cultural property, "free culture" movements in recent years have argued for broader access to and circulation of cultural forms, as well as creative rights to adapt and recombine them. Public humanities projects have promoted the digitization of archival materials and platforms for open access to them. These self-proclaimed progressive movements repeat the violence of colonial acquisition and circulation of Indigenous culture.

In the latter decades of the 20th century, Indigenous cultures were often invoked as the international framework for protecting heritage shifted from physical, monumental heritage to intangible cultural practices. But the recognition of "Intangible Cultural Heritage of Humanity" by UNESCO suggested that traditional cultures (Indigenous and otherwise) constituted the heritage of all humanity, thereby appropriating Indigenous knowledge for everyone else. This logic follows the assumptions of 19th century sociocultural evolutionism, according to which Indigenous peoples represented earlier stages of humanity—in other words, they were considered the ancestors of urban non-Indigenous people living at the very same time. This scientific racism still emerges in professional journalism and some parts of academia that seek out the origins of humanity in present day Indigenous groups. Heritage professionals should be vigilant in challenging, rather than reproducing, these problematic assumptions.

The emphasis on preservation in the international system and in museum/archive practices has had ambivalent results for Indigenous peoples. In the international system, mandating preservation led to the privileging of non-Indigenous experts who followed their own cultural protocols (dominant museum/archival practices) in the treatment of Indigenous materials. The "development" promised was often a development of neoliberal economic structures, rather than an increased control of Indigenous peoples over their cultures, governance and their children's futures. Physical sites became tourist attractions while Indigenous music and ceremonies became shows for gawking travelers.

Preservationist policies should be subjected to scrutiny and developed in collaboration with Indigenous communities. For whom are recordings/objects being preserved, and why? Asking these kinds of questions is imperative but can spark strong reactions from museum and archive professionals. Historically, preservation of music recordings was often accomplished at the expense of the communities who created the music. Francis Densmore, for example, made recordings of Native American music on behalf of the Smithsonian in the early 20th century, at the same time that she lobbied in Washington for the dissolution of tribal lands.[1] Without excusing these violations, Native Americans have reclaimed some recordings of their music, working together with institutions such as the Library of Congress Federal Cylinder Project. Putting these recordings to new uses, tribal members recovered songs that had been forbidden by missionaries and boarding schools and began to creatively restore gaps in cross-generational transmission.

The Ts'msyen scholar Robin Gray has powerfully argued that institutions holding "captured forms of in/tangible cultural heritage" should follow Indigenous customary law, rather than dominant intellectual property law, in determining the future of Indigenous materials.[2] This requires deep relationships of collaboration, co-leadership by Indigenous communities and their governments, as well as the transfer of rights, rather than simply making copies to hand out in the name of supposed "repatriation." The dominant legal status of Indigenous cultural property has already begun to shift since the 1990 Native American Graves Protection and Repatriation Act, which applies to sacred objects as well as human remains held by U.S. institutions with federal funding. The 2007 United Nations Declaration on the Rights of Indigenous Peoples explicitly links Indigenous heritage to intellectual property rights in Article 31:

> "Indigenous peoples have the right to maintain, control, protect and develop their cultural heritage, traditional knowledge

---

[1] Troutman, John. 2009. *Indian Blues: American Indians and the Politics of Music, 1879-1934.* Norman: University of Oklahoma Press.

[2] Gray, Robin. 2015. *Ts'msyen Revolution: The Poetics and Politics of Reclaiming.* Ph.D. Dissertation, University of Massachusetts, Amherst. P. 123.

and traditional cultural expressions, as well as the manifesta-
tions of their sciences, technologies and cultures, including human and genetic resources, seeds, medicines, knowledge of the
properties of fauna and flora, oral traditions, literatures, designs, sports and traditional games and visual and performing
arts. They also have the right to maintain, control, protect and
develop their intellectual property over such cultural heritage,
traditional knowledge, and traditional cultural expressions."

Though non-binding, the Declaration is an important legal resource for Indigenous peoples taking action against governments, corporations, or educational institutions to reclaim their cultural and intellectual property.[3]

Heritage professionals such as curators and archivists have their own
deeply embedded cultural practices that can be difficult to examine from
within their institutions and world views. The power of Heritage Studies
is to connect practical institutional work with critical analysis, opening up
professional paradigms to marginalized perspectives, including those of
Indigenous peoples and others who were objectified by museum sciences.
This requires shedding the strictures of inherited institutional order to begin real, messy dialogue with the people whose own pasts are represented
in museum and archive collections.

---

[3] For other useful resources, see Jane Anderson and Kim Christen's "Local Contexts" project
website (http://localcontexts.org/) and Trevor Reed's (2016) article "Who Owns Our Ancestors' Voices? Tribal Claims to Pre-1972 Sound Recordings," *Columbia Journal of Law and the
Arts* 40:275-310.

Daniel Maher: Folklore of the Tallgrass Prairie

As an anthropologist I study cultural heritage tourism sites. My present focus is on locations existing within the ecological zone of the tallgrass prairie as it existed circa 1800, stretching 1700 miles north to south from Winnipeg, Manitoba, to Corpus Christi, Texas, and 700 miles east to west from Lafayette, Indiana to Grand Island, Nebraska. Only a fraction of a percent of this original ecosystem exists today, but within it, hundreds of cultural heritage sites offer competing and often contesting narratives explaining to tourists what the human relationship to this land has been. Each site alone has a trove of folklore and is worthy of detailed analysis. From an anthropological perspective I am interested in what the overall collection of narratives says about this space, how the stories articulate American cultural values. The sites I have identified cluster into five broad themes of: natural restoration and preservation of tallgrass prairie and bison, historical pioneer narrative preservation, genetic seed preservation, counter-pioneer narratives, and best-land-use narratives.

The tallgrass prairie and bison sites range from Pawhuska, Oklahoma, to Strong City, Kansas, from three sites in Iowa – Des Moines, West Branch, and Decorah, to Wilmington, Illinois, as well as to three Aldo Leopold sites in, Burlington, Iowa, and Madison and Baraboo, Wisconsin. Leopold is a larger than life conservation folk hero and widely cited within the tallgrass prairie restoration movement. The story told at all these sites is one of returning the land to its original, pristine form before its devastation by the steel plow.

Frequently adjacent to these prairie restoration sites can be found pioneer sites that glorify the way of life that destroyed the tallgrass prairie. Most notably, sites associated with *Little House on the Prairie* dot the landscape between remnants of tallgrass prairie from Pepin, Wisconsin to Burr Oak, Iowa, from Walnut Grove Minnesota, to De Smet, South Dakota, from

Independence, Kansas, to Mansfield, Missouri. Between the locales of this Ingalls Wilder family-trek can be found hundreds of pioneer villages, pioneer museums, and founders/pioneer/heritage day events celebrating the conquest of the tallgrass prairie in the late nineteenth century.

Laced over these narratives are two distinct story lines that each emphasize a return to genetically pure seeds. On the one hand, organizations such as Seed Savers Exchange Farm, north of Decorah, Iowa, and Baker Creek Farms, north of Mansfield, Missouri, peddle heirloom seeds and stories to organic gardeners, back-to-the-landers, and other anti-agricorps groups and individuals. Both of these establishments expose the evils of corporate farming and provide the soothing solution of genetically pure seeds. On the other hand, Indian Nations from the Cherokee in Tahlequah, Oklahoma, to the Meskwaki in Tama, Iowa, advocate a return to indigenous seeds in food sovereignty initiative narratives. Genetically pure seeds in both these cases hold the key to resisting the encroachment of modernity.

The tallgrass prairie is also home to less popular and lesser known pioneer narratives. This is the space the Mormon Trail traverses, starting on the edge of the Mississippi in Carthage and Nauvoo, Illinois. Between Des Moines and Cedar Falls one can visit the Amana Colonies and immerse oneself in the vestiges of the Inspirationalists — a nineteenth century agrarian, communally organized, religious sect which is now a capitalist, tourist-focused, community plying generic Bavarian cultural experiences. From Decorah, Iowa to Minneapolis, Minnesota, Scandinavian pioneer stories dominate. The Vesterheim Norweigian-American heritage museum in Decorah is a stellar example of this narrative. Religious sects and specific ethnic pioneer narratives, while infinitely fascinating, seldom capture a wide American audience.

Contemporary narratives contesting best-land-use narratives also flourish within the tallgrass prairie. This is the home of Archer Daniels Midland (ADM), of Monsanto, and many other agribusiness corporations creating designer hybrid seeds (GMOs) and artificial fertilizers that will "feed the world." Narratives resisting these practices can be found in the next field over, however, at Joia Food Farm in Charles City, Iowa, or in the documentary *King Corn* filmed in Greene, Iowa, as well as at Seed Savers and Baker Creek farms.

What might we glean from an overall analysis of the narratives told to the folk within these five themes? Age old anthropological points of power, gender, and race come to the fore.

Tallgrass prairie and bison restoration and preservation sites frequently offer romanticized notions of Indian Nations living in peace, harmony, and tranquility within the tallgrass ecosystem. The picture painted of life before European arrival is one of virgin land, unchanged by human presence. This is simply not possible. Wherever humans live, even if they are foraging, they will change the ecosystem by selecting and deselecting specific plants and animals to eat or not eat.

The *Little House* story line reinforces the long-central American household values of boot-strap individualism coupled with heterosexual normativity. Akin to the John Wayne frontier narratives acting as a cultural foil to the Cold War, the entrance of Laura Ingalls Wilder stories onto American television in 1974 gave a country wearied with the Vietnam War a refuge, a home to return to, a veritable model for value-recalibration. Is it any wonder that the agrarian commune story of the Amana colonies with collective group homes and kitchens does not resonate?

Talk of genetic purity demands some close attention. What are heirloom seeds? What are indigenous plants? Animals? How do we know? When do we start time? What the plants and animals were in 1592, or 1776, or 2018, are not what the plants and animals were 10,000 years ago. To declare indigeneity – whether of people, plants, or animals — is to throw down an arbitrary staring point in time, a point which eclipses all that came before it. That being said, the Cherokee, the Meskwaki, and many other Indian Nations seek to return to a foodway of life that existed before European contact. What should we make of Baker Creek Farms and Seed Savers Exchange questing for heirloom seeds? An heirloom seed is not genetically altered. The offspring of an heirloom plant will produce seeds that will grow plants just like its parent. Hybrid seeds, on the other hand, will quickly lose their genetic composition if left to their own devices.

The fecundity of the tallgrass prairie has wrought wide-ranging folk narratives. Within this one ecological region people with quite varying religious, political, and economic vantage points can all find some story line that will reinforce their values. Those who look closely might experience what C. Wright Mills called a transvaluation of values. But vacationing tourists are seldom interested in sorting out the cognitive dissonance.

Barry Bergey: Cultural Diversity, Cultural Equity, and Commerce

[*The following plenary address was delivered by the former Director of the NEA Folk and Traditional Arts program, Barry Bergey, at the Experts Seminar on Cultural Diversity, Organization of American States, Vancouver, Canada, March 19, 2002. Bergey served as specialist at the NEA for 29 years, and directed its Folk and Traditional Arts program from 2000-2014.*]

In his 1977 *Appeal for Cultural Equity* folklorist and ethnomusicologist Alan Lomax warned of a "cultural grey-out," a loss of cultural distinctiveness and artistic variety worldwide due to the rapid globalization of culture and commerce. He later observed that if this trend continued "pretty soon there will be no place in the world left that's worth visiting – and no particular reason to stay home either." More recently, Christopher Clausen, in his book *Faded Mosaic: The Emergence of Post-Cultural America*, points out that the United States has become a country of "individualism without much individuality."

While cultural grey-out, or the fading of cultural distinctiveness, may still be a national, and indeed international issue, we have also learned that rumors of the death of cultural diversity have been somewhat premature. World musics, international films, ethnically distinct crafts have all become part of the global marketplace. The general mobility of world citizenry has brought peoples of different cultures into more frequent contact. Economic and political disruptions in a number of developing countries have led to cultural and geographic resettlements and an ongoing process of cultural adaptation and acclimation in our Hemisphere. The formation of new immigrant communities within nations has often led to a heightened consciousness of national and cultural identity and a more determined search on the part of immigrants for strategies of cultural maintenance as they adapt to new geographic and social environments.

Culturally distinct communities are not only affected by the global marketplace, they have often, whether willingly or unwilling, found themselves participating in that marketplace. *Safeguarding Traditional Cultures: A Global Assessment*, published jointly by UNESCO and the Smithsonian Institution, points out:

> Many businesses today create wealth using the forms and materials of traditional cultures – local cooperatives that produce and market handmade crafts, industrial textile manufacturers that employ traditional designs, producers of audio recordings of traditional music, pharmaceutical manufacturers that use indigenous knowledge of healing plants, promoters of tourism, and entertainment conglomerates that employ various forms of ethnic representations for motion pictures, amusement theme parks, and children's toys. This large commercial sector has developed ways of dealing with folklore and traditional culture that affect their production, dissemination, and preservation.

An equally profound change affecting culture and commerce has come with the development of new technologies. In recent years there has been a shifting relationship between the makers and performers of art and the audiences for artistic work. While we used to think that the medium had become the message, it seems that now the medium is rapidly consuming both the message and the messenger. New technologies such as the Internet, cable and satellite broadcast, and sophisticated optical copying instruments, have de-linked the creator and the consumer. Corporate consolidation has further alienated the distributors of cultural products — the record, film, and media companies — from both the artists and the consumers. As our products of popular culture have become, over time, associated with our national identity and perceived as our cultural patrimony, there has also been a concern over how multinational corporations address issues of conservation of and access to seminal cultural products, such as masters of recordings, visual images, film, and video.

Pixels, bytes, ROMs, and RAMs recognize no national boundaries and respect no legal constraints. Organizations such as the Recording Industry Association of America (RIAA) and the International Intellectual Property Alliance (IIPA) have offered startling statistics about the piracy of intellectual and cultural material. An IIPA study estimates that in 2001 copyright piracy produced a total loss of $8,379,700,000 in the following areas: motion pictures - $1.288 billion; sound recordings and musical compositions -

$2.034 billion; business software applications - $2.6535 billion; entertainment software – $1.7671 billion; and books – $636.4 million. In the area of music alone, it is estimated that 3.6 billion songs are illegally downloaded each month. In recent testimony before the Committee on Commerce, Science and Transportation of the U.S. Senate, Hilary Rosen, President and CEO of RIAA, acknowledged that attempts by the music industry to develop technological protections from piracy have largely failed. New technologies to circumvent the protections have to this point been implemented as fast as new safeguards have been developed.

Successful recording artists and theatrical film actors have also become more vocal about how the new technologies and corporate consolidation have impinged on their ability to earn fair remuneration for their efforts. A recently formed organization, the Recording Artists Coalition, has taken stands on such issues as Internet rights, work for hire, payola, contract length, and contract stipulations, as they affect individual artists.

It appears that the combination of new technologies and corporate consolidation have created a three-way disenfranchisement, separating and in some cases placing at odds, the creators of culture, the conveyors of culture, and the consumers of culture. Ironically, the piracy of cultural products often places the very audiences for cultural content at odds with both the artists and the distributors of cultural material. The social contract that has historically been reflected in loyalty to individual artists and realized in consumer patronage of aesthetic and stylistic traditions that are rooted in and reflective of regional, national or cultural identity, has in a sense been broken. The U.S. Supreme Court has recently agreed to consider a challenge to the 1998 law extending copyright protection from 50 to 70 years, because many argue that this extension impinges on First Amendment rights and does not serve the common good.

I do not offer a solution for these pervasive and profoundly difficult problems. Working in a small federal agency in the United States Government that deals mainly with the not-for-profit cultural sector, I feel ill-prepared to offer advice about how either nations or the commercial cultural industry might address these important issues. Further, working with folk and traditional arts as I do, I'm afraid that our sector, while diverse in character and ubiquitous in practice, does not benefit from the infrastructural mechanisms adequate to turn the tide of cultural and commercial development.

I can however offer my personal opinion that governmental agencies and ministries of culture may need to consider whether their legal and enforcement instruments are at this point capable of legislating or enforcing either cultural diversity or commercial fair-play in the national and international marketplace. Nations may be faced with the choice of whether to invest their fiscal and legal resources to address issues of cultural ownership or cultural stewardship. In the not-for-profit arts sector, with which I am most familiar, we have found that there are a number of strategies for proactively encouraging aesthetic diversity and cultural self-determination. While respecting cultural ownership, it is the area of cultural stewardship that offers the potential for providing systemic solutions to problems of loss of tradition, aesthetic conflation, and cultural enervation.

I would assert a few basic principles of cultural stewardship: 1) a community, a region, or a nation will benefit from the identification, documentation and conservation of its cultural resources; 2) artistic, linguistic, and cultural diversity will contribute to a vibrant society; 3) transmission and nurturance of artistic skills, local knowledge, and community-based values are key to conserving cultural memory and to building a sustainable future; and 4) respect for and celebration of individual ways of knowing, doing, and being, as reflected in community consultation and local collaboration, will most effectively sustain artistic heritage, ensure social health, and protect cultural wealth.

The National Endowment for the Arts has undertaken the support of the folk and traditional arts through a multi-faceted funding strategy that includes funding of programs and projects in the following areas: 1) discovery – fieldwork that identifies and documents artistic and cultural resources; 2) education – transmission of artistic skills, as well as education in and about diverse cultural traditions; 3) celebration and presentation – performance programs, media productions, and exhibitions presenting artistic work; 4) protection – support for programs that safeguard culturally significant work, structures, landscapes and communities; 5) infrastructure – building cultural expertise and organizational capacity to support traditional artists.

Funding through our agency, while modest in amount, is aimed at supporting a wide variety of programs and projects that address these strategies. Included in our funding is the targeted support for statewide local and regional survey and documentation projects; development of an infrastructure of cultural specialists at the state, local and regional level; funding of statewide folk arts apprenticeship programs to encourage the transmission of artistic skills and knowledge; and the recognition of individual artists through the National Heritage Fellowships, an award honoring master traditional artists.

While these funding programs have been modestly successful, I often encounter several popular misperceptions about folk and traditional arts.

First, tradition is often perceived as about the past, not the future. This presents a false choice. In a healthy cultural context, tradition is what builds the future. Tradition bearers carry cultural knowledge and artistic skills of relevance to contemporary society. As one of our writers of the American South, William Faulkner, has said, "The past is not dead, it is not even past yet." Culture is organic in nature and, in order for it to survive, growth and development are necessary. Preservation, a term that might bear further discussion, is not about pickling or embalming culture, rather it is about nourishing or nurturing living cultural practice. In many Native American communities today there is a neo-traditional movement that involves a return to traditional values and practices among youth in order to address some of the significant societal problems confronting young people, including alcoholism, drug abuse, and suicide. In some of those same communities you are as likely to find artists beading beautiful designs on tennis shoes or baseball caps as on traditional regalia. The focus of this cultural revitalization is today, not yesterday.

Second, on a related topic, it is often thought that tradition is about imitation and reproduction and not innovation and creation. This only serves to undervalue the contributions of folk artists. Traditional artists continually bring fresh perspectives and experiences to their work. One of the incredibly interesting things about traditional arts is that there is so much aesthetic variation in the work, as reflected by varying regional or cultural contexts. Often operating outside of formalized systems, traditional or folk arts frequently benefit from the freedom to bring new perspectives to the artistic process. In the United States we see immigrant Hmong (Miao) needleworkers making pillowcases and bed-covers using western color schemes for an American market, in addition to the traditional colors and styles that might be used for personal clothing. The tradition of patchwork quilting demonstrates a wide variety of aesthetic styles as reflected in the ingenious work of European American, Native American, Native Hawaiian, and African American artists. There are many forks along the pathway of tradition.

Third, it is often thought that tradition is preserved in isolation, removed from cultural contact and interchange. Many ethnographers in the United States during the early 20th century journeyed to remote rural areas and to Native American reservations to document what they thought would be the purest forms of traditional arts. We now realize that the folk and traditional arts do not depend on isolation to survive; on the contrary, folk arts often spring up and flourish in areas where there is either new or ongoing cultural contact. Highways and railways carried musical and material culture traditions to new geographic areas and produced new artistic styles and traditions.

In the United States, traditional music in the sparsely settled Appalachian mountains was, as early as the mid-nineteenth century, incorporating instrumentation and vocal characteristics drawn from African, Anglo, Celtic, and European traditions. Musical traditions such as jazz emerged in the early twentieth century in cultural crossroads such as New Orleans, combining elements of African American, Afro-Caribbean, and European cultures. Cities such as Chicago, Memphis, and Nashville have brought together new immigrants or migrant populations and have served as epicenters for new popular musical forms such as urban blues, country and western, and rock and roll. Technological innovations such as radio broadcast and recordings spread distinct regional musical traditions to broader audiences, often producing a florescence of new artistic activity. Cultural contact and aesthetic sharing, or should we say borrowing, have been ongoing aspects of grassroots artistic history.

Finally, a common misperception is that tradition is always about the "other" and not about "us." Tradition is not served well when we think of it as exotic, as quaint, or as primitive, that is, as removed from us in time or space or social circumstance. Until we appreciate the role that art, culture, and tradition play in our own lives, it will be difficult for us to conceive of an integrated approach to cultural policy. The creative impulse, respect for time-tested knowledge and skills, and an affinity for cultivating and occupying common cultural ground all seem to be part, at least, of what defines us as humans. When our cultural policies and practices address some of these universal issues, we will have improved our potential to provide a constructive foundation for living cultural heritage.

When it comes to the global marketplace, I still have to remind myself that the pop cultural sector of our economy far outweighs the not for profit domain that I interact with day to day. In fact, one might say that mass culture is the 500-pound gorilla with Attention Deficit Disorder at the tea party. For instance, the copyright industries that involve cultural products represented $457.2 billion, or 4.9% of the GDP, in 1999. The budget of the National Endowment for the Arts is just a little over $100 million. John Seabrook in *Nobrow: The Culture of Marketing – The Marketing of Culture* argues that popular culture has flattened the old high and low culture hierarchy, substituting acts of appetite for acts of taste. The mass marketplace feeds a very hungry gorilla.

We ignore the power of the marketplace at our own peril. How do we find a way to wed the energy and strength of the open market with the mission and ideals of a civil society that cares about aesthetic democracy and cultural continuity? How do we enhance appreciation of diverse aesthetic and cultural traditions? How do we reconnect artists with audiences? How do we encourage respect for intellectual property? I would suggest that these are questions that both the commercial and the not for profit sector must answer. On purely practical terms, I doubt that these answers can be legislated. I do think, however, that we can nurture from within what it is impossible to control from without. This will require both national resolve and international cooperation. A key factor will be the cultivation of respect for each individual nation's diverse cultural assets.

There also are opportunities for the commercial and non-commercial segments of our societies to find common cause and to learn from one another. In marketing cultural products, commercial companies might follow the lead of nonprofit cultural organizations and provide value-added materials, such as interpretive writing, visual design features, and supplementary historical or archival materials, with sound recordings and digital video items so that downloaded digital bits will not be a substitute for the total cultural product. Both the commercial and non-commercial sectors can re-value and re-affirm the importance of artistic creation, of cultural education, of aesthetic diversity, and of local, regional and national artistic assets in our individual and collective lives. The commercial cultural sector can work toward the commitment of a portion of royalties, or of profits on public domain materials, to projects and programs that support our nation's artistic assets and cultural legacy. Both sectors can re-connect artists and audiences through affirming the primacy of the first-hand artistic experience, whether it be through live performance or theatrical presentation of film. The benefits of new technologies developed for the commercial market can provide access for nonprofits to new audiences and can serve niche markets that are culturally or geographically removed from the mainstream. Both the commercial and the non-commercial sectors can encourage international cultural exchange through reciprocal tours of performing artists or exhibitions, sharing of media programs that speak to national cultural identity, and joint meetings of cultural and business leaders.

A recent publication by the Center for Arts and Culture entitled *Preserving Our Heritage* points out that "Cultural preservation, like the conservation of our natural resources, depends upon political leadership, the resources of civil society, and the popular will." Both biological and cultural diversity represent issues that connect the nations of our Hemisphere in ways that transcend political, social, and geographic boundaries. I continue to hope that the citizenry within our respective countries will see that conservation of cultural vitality and diversity is as important to our well being as is responsible care for our natural environment. Meetings such as this provide a welcome opportunity to continue the ever-timely cultural conversation about cultural conservation.

Cherisse Jones-Branch: Heritage Studies and Local History: "Whose Heritage?"

Exploring Heritage Studies from a local perspective requires a deep and thoughtful consideration of who has the right to interpret and control access to representations of the past. It has often depended upon those who were politically connected or those, as is the case in communities the world over, who were the landowning or class elite. But it has also included moments where its practitioners have shifted and changed narratives in ways that have made them more complicated, nuanced, inclusive, regional, and local. They have begged the question "Whose Heritage?" in their work.[1] In doing so, Heritage Studies practitioners have engaged in cultural and intellectual work that has unearthed stories that have resisted and in fact upturned traditional understandings of place and space. This approach considers sources that are often not found in traditional archives and repositories. Once unburied, they provide a unique way of interpreting and understanding a place's heritage from a perspective few have previously considered valuable or useful. They reveal much about how marginalized groups, in their own way, have asked and answered the question, "Whose Heritage?" I have employed this particular framework to explore the local history of African American women in the rural Mississippi Valley region and in Arkansas in particular between 1913 and 1972. The scholarship I have produced over the past five years upends

---

[1] Graham Fairclough, Rodney Harrison, John H. Jameson Jr., and John Schofield, editors, *The Heritage Reader* (New York: Routledge: 2008), 8.

that which has either ignored rural black women altogether or has only analyzed them as beleaguered agricultural laborers.

Rural spaces have long been imagined in idyllic terms. Locality informed memories of these spaces as being close knit and relatively free of turmoil. They have also been cast as predominantly white environments that were neatly ordered according to a very strict racial hierarchy to which there was allegedly very little resistance. When viewed through the lens of race and gender however, rural spaces read very differently. Arkansas between 1913 and 1972, like all of the South during this period, was mapped as a very white and hyper-masculine place. Extant sources, again, found in traditional archives and repositories, reveal this very clearly. However, what happens when one excavates sources outside of those environs? How does the history and heritage change? And how does this change long standing and accepted narratives?

What I can say affirmatively is that when the lens and sources used for heritage studies analysis changes, so too does the locality's social, political, and economic ethnoscape.[2] Consider, for instance, the Arkansas Delta. Scholars have written extensively about massive white landownership and agricultural production.[3] They have also given a nod to the predominantly African American communities that labored in this area for generations. However, when the focus is placed upon black landownership in this space, the narrative and thus its heritage look very different. For instance, what did it mean that between 1870-1910, over two hundred thousand African Americans migrated to Arkansas in search of land and improved economic and political opportunities? Indeed, black migration to the state outpaced white migration. Furthermore, in 1870, the largest percentage of black landowners in the South resided in Arkansas. The Arkansas Republican Party promoted black migration to the state, and African Americans sought, obtained, and maintained political power in the earliest years of the twentieth century.[4]

But what does this look like when viewed through a gendered lens? That is, how does the condition of locality help one parse out black women's lives in rural Arkansas? How does Heritage Studies help us better and more accurately place them within agricultural history? These are the questions which guided my research when my interests turned to exploring rural women's history.

---

[2]Fairclough, 181

[3]See Jeannie Whayne, *Delta Empire: Lee Wilson and the Transformation of Agriculture in the New South* (Baton Rouge: Louisiana State University Press, 2011).

[4]Story Matkin-Rawn, "The Great Negro State of the Country: Arkansas's Reconstruction and the Other Great Migration," *Arkansas Historical Quarterly,* 72, no. 1 (Spring 2013): 2, 3, 12, 15, 16.

A closer look at black women's lives in rural communities quickly reveals that they were educators, landowners, and even politicians. In Arkansas and the Mississippi Valley region, many rural black women were employed as Jeanes Supervising Industrial Teachers. Supported by an endowment left in 1907 by Anna T. Jeanes, a Pennsylvania Quaker, "Jeanes Supervisors" worked to improve the quality of educational access in rural black communities from 1909-1968.[5] An emphasis on predominantly white schools in these spaces or even the integration of public schools beginning after the 1954 *Brown v. Board of Education* Supreme Court decision has traditionally marginalized the significance of Jeanes Supervisors in the communities in which they lived and labored. Reading and exploring against the grain of mainstream stories in these spaces allows one to uncover African Americans' resourcefulness and hopefulness despite the racial injustice they endured daily.[6]

While scholars have focused largely on white, and to a lesser extent, black male southern landowners, few would imagine that black women have their own stories to tell about landownership. Reimagining the race and gender of landowners as black and female compels a reconsideration of culture in the Arkansas Delta. One such example is Marvell, Arkansas's Annie Zachary Pike who was born in 1930 in rural Phillips County. In 1952, she married Grover C. Zachary, an African American landowner who employed black tenants. After he became ill, his wife assumed the responsibility for the family farm. Annie Zachary Pike (she remarried in 1977 after her first husband died in 1973,) was also a well-known community activist who served on the United States Department of Agriculture's Citizens Advisory Committee on Civil Rights and in 1972 ran for the Arkansas State Senate as a Republican.[7]

Heritage work in local communities profoundly changes historical narratives. When the voices and stories of the marginalized and unrepresented are uncovered and included as a part of Heritage Studies practitioners' efforts, it only deepens the local culture's richness and texture. It reveals a multiplicity of opinions about and reactions to heritage and its different meanings. Studying local heritage in this way further tells us much about how differently people understand and in the past have un-

---

[5]The Arkansas Jeanes Supervisor program only lasted until 1950.

[6]For more information about Jeanes Supervisors, see Adam Fairclough, *Teaching Equality: Black Schools in the Age of Jim Crow* (Athens: University of Georgia Press, 2001); *Black Teachers in the Segregated South: A Class of Their Own* (Cambridge: Belknap Press, 2007), and Phyllis McClure, *Jeanes Teachers: A View into Black Education in the Jim Crow South* (Charleston, S.C.: BookSurge Publishing, 2009).

[7]Cherisse Jones-Branch, "Been a Guinea Pig in this Race: Annie Ruth Zachary Pike, Arkansas Homemaker, Farmer, and Politician," *International Journal of Africana Studies*, 19, no. 1 (Spring-Summer 2018): 7-24.

derstood the landscape they are very much a part of. Their experiences inspire much needed curiosity. And their insights are crucial to fully expli- cating the history of place, space, and memory. This level of inclusiveness thus allows them to critically engage the question, "Whose Heritage?"

Betsy H. Bradley: Critical Heritage and Historic Preservation: "Scanning the Field and Looking Ahead"

The 2016 celebration of the fiftieth anniversary of the passage of the National Historic Preservation Act of 1966 prompted the review of programs and policies. More importantly, it brought to the forefront how many historic preservationists feel a sense of dissatisfaction and angst about how practice is likely to proceed during the next decades of historic, or heritage, preservation of the built environment. A contingent of preservationists that remains most interested in iconic architectural and historic properties considers the American programs and national policies to be working well. However, many practitioners, mainly those working at the local level and with community groups, are not so sure. For us, the field of critical heritage studies provides an integrated intellectual and practice-oriented means to explore new directions for the field.

Anyone familiar with American policies and practices in historic preservation identifies instantly with Laurajane Smith's term (2006:29) "authorized heritage discourse (AHD)." Indeed, historic preservation has a conceptual and action-governing infrastructure more dominant than other components of heritage work in the United States. This infrastructure, or AHD, guides how we evaluate historic significance, designate local, state and national historic sites on official lists, and undertake design review of alterations to historic buildings and in historic districts. Current policies

and practices are based on poorly-articulated theories about historic significance and historic integrity even as they are explained in prescriptive
detail. Because our AHD is powerful and remains largely unchallenged,
we must ask: is the strong center supported by our AHD worthy of its
reach and consequences? And we must answer: No, then proceed with
the understanding that while it is unlikely that laws and policies will soon
be altered, practice is the vehicle through which change can be realized.

We must approach the future and develop revised practices by first recognizing that the American program is uncomfortably situated, with direction from the national level being delivered as "best practices" – with one
approach for each task, often delivered without any adaptation for local
conditions and needs in places from deep rural counties to large cities.[1]
Two theoretical constructs expose this discomfort. First, the concept of
"best practices" framed at the national level is a false one, as no one small
group of practices can address the immensely complex array of communities and their interests in the United States. As we ask, "Best for whom?"
we realize the strong relationship between the group powerful enough to
establish a government program and policies and the group it best serves.
We should strive to develop an array of effective practices that are project
and location specific.

Another aspect of this discomfort stems from the unnecessarily hardened structural reach of our AHD, which we might most usefully think of
as a conceptual and informational infrastructure.[2] Many fields have such
frameworks that enable people to work together across lines of authority, roles and geography by supplying a common language and practices.
Such infrastructures seem to be all-inclusive, as demonstrated by the way
we categorize historic resources as eligible or not eligible, contributing
or non-contributing. These categories are predicated on an unexamined
understanding that all those involved concur with the theory underlying
the use of these particular categories. The infrastructures of other fields,
medicine for instance, demonstrate that these conceptual and action-based
infrastructures can be, and sometimes are, revised. They are modified in
small ways to respond to new information and revised understandings.
Thinking about our national historic preservation program in this manner

---

[1]My critique of best practices has benefitted from Gretchen Rumohr-Voskuil's commen-
tary, "Best Practice: Past, Present and Personal" as well as from standard feminist theory that
asks, "For whom?"

[2]Bowker and Star explain the functions of conceptual infrastructures through the lens of
sociology and communication in a way that is contextual for LauraJane Smith's identification
and unpacking of an Authorized Heritage Discourse. Bowker and Star highlight the functions
of classification and use various aspects of medicine to demonstrate their arguments. Chapter
1, in particular Table 1.1, defines a conceptual infrastructure and its classification work.

— rather than as a set of hardened practices that are spoken of as official policies — will foster the development of new categories, approaches, and ways of understanding at the local level where the ill-fitting mandates of a national infrastructure are revealed.

The "historic district" concept affords opportunities for consideration of more robust practice theories. While Americans visit iconic landmarks and historic sites, they live in communities and neighborhoods of various ages. These more everyday places have been addressed through the "historic district" concept: the identification of a discreet historic area and the management of change in it over time. Local historic districts provide recognition and protection of these areas through "historic district" designation, and regulation through the issuance of building permits. The results include neighborhoods where owner-occupied properties predominate, property values rise, and blocks of houses become stable neighborhoods – as well as districts in Legacy Cities where historic districts have been ravaged by disinvestment and loss of population.

The design review of regulation was developed as a means to maintain the historic integrity of each building as a component of a larger area that conveys a historic time and place. While successful in moderating physical change, historic districts present some challenges that have arisen over time, challenges that are not in the forefront of many conversations. My involvement in local historic districts in several locations prompts me to critique the level of detail that design review should address. I question the use of resources to continue to "curate" successful historic districts, as James Marston Fitch (1990:xiv) has described the work.[3] If all the buildings in a district have been restored and current changes proposed are minimal, indicating that the district has been recovered or is newly stabilized, then perhaps a second phase – without design review – could be possible and desirable.

Questioning of what is considered to be successful, but could be different, led me to a practice theory with which to think through my concerns and come to possible solutions. I am using Edward Relph's explanation of sense of place as the basis for formulating new practices.[4] Relph writes of

---

[3] Fitch, firmly embedded in the design and conservation aspects of the architectural component of historic preservation, uses a museum metaphor that refers to all aspects of the built environment as artifacts of various scales. This museum metaphor successfully highlights the contrast with new design and construction. However, Fitch's concern with the mass production of post-industrial artifacts keeps a focus on the prototypes and the most individual designs, rather than on the lived-in nature of historic districts that have not been removed from everyday use as curated artifacts. This inherent tension must be resolved, and the curatorial metaphor is likely not to address the interests of many preservationists.

[4] A cultural geographer with a phenomenological approach, Ned Relph has continued to explore placeness, place and placelessness on his blog < http://www.placeness.com > and

a setting, activity and meaning as the components of sense of place, the attachment that people develop to places where they spend time (1975:46-47). In a residential historic district, living is the activity that has meanings for identity and quality of life. In a district of commercial buildings, retail activity, use of upper floors for residential use, and new workplaces are often present with a mix of activities and meanings. If we recast our traditional concern with the built environment to be concern with a setting which is rich in history and design and intended to support activity and meaning — then perhaps we can relax about the effects of some proposed changes. The danger of "a slippery slope" introduced by one less authentic building element or material has less sway when we consider historic districts through a Relphian lens. Commons theory should also be useful when we examine our historic district programs. It is the unstated underlying understanding that property owners in the district share a valued, finite resource. Commons governance could support theorizing about a combinations of city officials, boards, and community organization oversight that varies over time.[5]

If we think of heritage as a process, as LauraJane Smith (2006:44) asserts, then our process in the United States is incomplete because it stops after properties are brought into the collection of heritage resources to be managed. Practice theories will be important as we initiate conversations about ways to move to a Phase Two, or the sunsetting of some historic preservation programs, or the removal of properties from those programs. The success of local historic districts comes with costs and unintended consequences. The displacement of people as property values rise, known as gentrification, is an unintended effect that we assign to the forces of the market place but nevertheless decry. City employees end up literally curating neighborhoods for wealthy property owners. Buildings long vacant and nearly ruinous are approved for demolition in Legacy City historic districts as there is no prospect of rehabilitation and re-occupancy. With no discussion of how to address both success and failure in historic districts, these conditions are unlikely to change. Relph reminds us that we know intellectually that places change over time in all respects, but the emotional attachment to place and devotion to permanency supports clinging to unchanged buildings and unchanging programs. We now know also that some historic places will be affected by climate change conditions that cannot be held off, and we must consider more scenarios for the future. Our many historic districts can serve as laboratories as we begin

---

has provided additional ways to work with place using a pragmatic, dynamic approach.

[5]Bollier's work on Commons theory and relating it to contemporary life has been influential.

to discuss, experiment with, and negotiate how our existing policies and practices need to be more flexible.

Critical heritage studies provides a framework and mandate for forward-looking practitioners in historic preservation to reveal and critique the relationships between theory and practice. Hugh T. Miller reminds us that "Practice is the theory in place; theory is the next-to-be practice." (2002:54-55) Turning to robust theory tied directly to addressing people's relationships to place, as well as others further afield, can be a means for revising practice by incorporating intellectual rigor and cross-disciplinary study. We need to broaden our sense of expertise to support the projects of community groups and residents, projects which are likely to be different from ones we have previously implemented. We need to be open to various ways of knowing places, and most of all, to the meanings that places have to various people. We need to adopt a realistic vision for the scope and length of programs, and be willing to redirect resources once our work has been successful. We have avoided discussing failures, particularly in Legacy City situations. But as we grapple with impending effects of climate change and migration, we must become reconciled to the fact that our programs may have horizons, and we must understand what that means for our current work. In order to undertake these mandates, we need to expand our interdisciplinary reach and contemplate theories about heritage, culture, the relationships between people and the built environment. If we do all this, critical heritage studies will have served us well and we can look to a different future for understanding the built environment during the next fifty years.

References

Bollier, David. 2014. *Think Like a Commoner.* New Society Publishers.

Bowker, Geoffrey C and Susan Leigh Star. 1999. *Sorting Things Out: Classification and its Consequences.* Cambridge, The MIT Press.

Fitch, James Marston. 1990. *Historic Preservation: Curatorial Management of the Built World.* New York: McGraw-Hill.

Miller, Hugh T. 2002. *Postmodern Public Policy.* Albany: State University of New York Press, 2002. Epub.

Relph, E. 1976. *Place and Placelessness.* London, Pion Limited.

Rumohr-Voskuil, Gretchen. 2010. Best Practice: Past, Present and Personal. *Language Arts Journal of Michigan* 25 (2):26-28.

Smith, LauraJane. 2006. *Uses of Heritage.* London and New York: Routledge.

Jeremy C. Wells: Folklore and Historic Preservation: "Building Bridges"

I was a graduate student in the historic preservation program at the University of Pennsylvania the first time I saw a reference to folklore and folklife. Back in 2004, I was looking for a doctoral program to continue my studies that explored the relationship between people and older (or "historic") places. Stumbling upon the web site for the now defunct Center for Folklore and Ethnography was an exhilarating experience: here was a doctoral program that attempted to understand people's relationship with old places using social science methods. This was (and continues to be) a novel focus in the academy. I found it curious that none of my professors in the historic preservation program even mentioned folklore, much less the Center that was right at our back door. Imagine my disappointment when I read further and discovered that the university was cancelling the doctoral program in folklore. While I found an alternate doctoral program that did allow me to pursue my research interests, this early experience left me wondering why there was no explicit relationship between folklore and historic preservation, given their similar interests. I will therefore attempt to explore some of the reasons for this apparent divide between these two fields and suggest some ways to bridge them.

The disciplinary roots of historic preservation lie primarily in positivistic strains of history, archaeology, and architecture.[1] The regulatory envi-

---

[1]Steven W. Semes, *The Future of the Past: A Conservation Ethic for Architecture, Urbanism, and Historic Preservation* (New York and London: W.W. Norton & Company, 2009); Jeremy C. Wells, "The Plurality of Truth in Culture, Context, and Heritage: A (mostly) Post-structuralist Analysis of Urban Conservation Charters," *City and Time* 3, no. 2:1 (2007): 1-13; Joseph A. Tainter and G. John Lucas, "Epistemology of the Significance Concept," *American Antiquity* 48, no. 4 (1983): 707-719; Howard L. Green, "The Social Construction of Historical Signifi-

ronment drives about three quarters of historic preservation practice, and these rules, laws, and regulations were mostly written by historians, although one particular rule, the Secretary of the Interior's Standards, was written by an architect.[2] Because so much of the work of historic preservation — mostly environmental review (Section 106 and NEPA) and design review (local historic districts and state and federal tax credit projects) — demands objectivity, which is enforced by law, its perspective is defined by expert rule and top-down processes that, by design, exclude local knowledge. Laurajane Smith has named this practice the "authorized heritage discourse" (AHD) in which the meanings and values of the public (non-experts) are actively "sidelined" so that experts maintain total control of the art/historical values demanded by preservation rules, laws, and regulations.[3]

Traditionally, academics have added little to the growth of historic preservation as a field beyond educating future practitioners; in other words, as Ned Kaufman describes it, functionally, there is no basic or applied research in higher education that serves to inform, improve, or better define historic preservation practice.[4] Indeed, it is quite common for historic preservation degree programs to have no full-time faculty and to rely entirely on adjuncts, who are typically well-qualified preservation practitioners. While frequently trained in the kind of interpretive/archival research methods used in local history, most of these practitioners are not trained in social science research methodologies, and are thus ill prepared as researchers in general. In addition, the unfortunate nature of adjuncts as second-class citizens in universities means that they do not have the same institutional support for research as do their full-time, tenure-track colleagues.

In comparison to historic preservation, folklore studies is mostly an academic endeavor, with far fewer applied, practice-based outlets, although the situation was not always this way. In the early 1980s, there was a brief period where folklore received equal treatment with historic preservation and archaeology from the National Park Service and state historic preservation offices. Indeed, the National Park Service and the National Folklife Center even added an amendment to the National Historic Preser-

---

cance," in *Preservation of What, for Whom? A Critical Look at Historical Significance*, edited by Michael A. Tomlan, 85-94 (Ithaca, NY: National Council for Preservation Education, 1998).

[2]National Park Service, "A History of The Secretary of the Interior's Standards," https://www.nps.gov/tps/standards/history-of-standards.htm.

[3]Laurajane Smith, *Uses of Heritage* (London: Routledge, 2006).

[4]Ned Kaufman, "Resistance to Research: Diagnosis and Treatment of a Disciplinary Ailment," in *Human-Centered Conservation: Theory and Evidence-Based Practice*, edited by Jeremy C. Wells and Barry L. Stiefel, 309-331 (London: Routledge, 2019).

vation Act authorizing a research report into the "intangible elements of our cultural heritage such as arts, skills, folklife and folkways."[5] State historic preservation offices began hiring employees to specialize in folklife and folklore; some states even made this a regulatory requirement. A number of important reports appeared during this time, such as *Cultural Conservation: The Protection of Cultural Heritage* by Ormond Loomis and *The Conservation of Culture: Folklorists and the Public Sector* by Burt Feintuch.[6] Folklorists produced many useful reports on the intangible heritage of various cultural groups during this era as well; but by the 1990s, interest in applied aspect of folklore that overlapped with historic preservation had pretty much disappeared, largely due to folklife researchers' increasing discomfort with the flawed agendas of a federal bureaucracy.[7] Since then, what has now become known as "cultural resource management" has failed to consider, much less use, ethnographic or social science perspectives.

More recently, in 2011, the American Folklore Society established the Folklore and Historic Preservation Policy Working Group, led by Laurie Sommers and Michael Ann Williams. In 2013, they released a whitepaper on "Integrating Folklore and Historic Preservation Policy: Toward a Richer Sense of Place."[8] Its initial recommendations largely focused on the way in which folklore could help in the creation of National Register nominations for traditional cultural properties (TCPs). TCP nominations, however, require the researcher to adopt the etic perspective in describing cultural meanings in an effort to satisfy regulatory requirements (and the AHD). For instance, if a cultural group believes a place to be significant because it is the location from which the creator of the Earth arose, it is entirely unacceptable to describe this from the perspective of the cultural group. (The criteria for a National Register nomination explicitly disallows statements of significance based on religious meanings, for instance.) Instead, one must adopt the etic perspective that objectively describes cultural activity from a detached perspective, such as "for thousands of years this cultural group has practiced ceremonies related to their belief system at this place." While the use of ethnographies in this way may result in more

---

[5]National Historic Preservation Act of 1966 (as amended), section 502.

[6]Ormond Loomis, *Cultural Conservation: The Protection of Cultural Heritage in the United States* (Washington, DC: American Folklife Center and the National Park Service, 1983); Burt Feintuch, *The Conservation of Culture: Folklorists and the Public Sector* (Lexington, KY: University Press of Kentucky, 1988).

[7]Richard Vidutis, "Missed Opportunities: The Absence of Ethnography in America's Cultural Heritage Programs," in *Human-Centered Conservation: Theory and Evidence-Based Practice*, edited by Jeremy C. Wells and Barry L. Stiefel, 255-272 (London: Routledge, 2019), 258.

[8]https://www.afsnet.org/page/FHPPolicyPaper

TCPs being nominated to the National Register, it perpetuates colonialism and continues to privilege Western, scientific understandings of reality.[9] In 2016, however, an update to this report found that, increasingly, discussions in historic preservation were moving toward a people-centered (or "humanistic") approach, more compatible with the ethnographic perspective that is an inherent part of folklore studies.

Any bridging of folklore and historic preservation will fail unless advocates for both fields recognize the massive influence that the regulatory environment has had on the practice of the latter. If Section 106, federal tax credit projects, and design review as part of local historic districts would disappear tomorrow, it would destroy the field; indeed, most of its practitioners would be unemployed. In this sense, historic preservation gains its legitimacy through force, or enforcement. And, most importantly, historic preservation cannot become significantly more people — or human — centric without changes to these laws. Few government agencies are willing to use taxpayer dollars to fund additional work that is not required by a rule or regulation. Yet there is little, if any, incentive to change these laws, to alter this political process. Most members of the public are not aware of this critical discourse which is happening within folklore studies and, increasingly, within the newly established field of critical heritage studies, a field which has adopted much of the perspective long used by folklore studies. Thus, the integration of folklore and historic preservation, while possible, must happen outside of the regulatory practices that are required by law; and this is a small space, indeed.

Perhaps the most fruitful area of collaboration is in interpretation. Historic site interpretation is often dry, too objective, and pedantic, especially from the perspective of the end user. Research in critical heritage studies is increasingly rejecting the notion that the main purpose of these sites is education, and researchers instead are focusing on how these places can be emotionally engaging and even cathartic for visitors.[10] The emic perspective offered by folklore could be an incredibly powerful way to engage the public in historic sites and increase their overall relevancy. Folklore could also be used, as is stated in the American Folklore Society's report, to help us understand what it is about historic (or simply older) places that are uniquely meaningful and important to people. This kind of basic social science research that focuses on the people/older place equation is altogether too rare, but it is essential for a more human-centric perspective

[9] See Rich Hutchings and Marina La Salle. "Archaeology as Disaster Capitalism," *International Journal of Historical Archaeology* 19 (2015): 699–720.

[10] Laurajane Smith and Gary Campbell, "The Elephant in the Room: Heritage Affect, and Emotion," in *A Companion to Heritage Studies*, Edited by William Logan, Máiréad Nic Craith and Ullrich Kockel, 443-460 (Chichester: Wiley-Blackwell, 2015).

on how we should conserve old places for the maximal benefit of people.

In sum, the more natural ally with folklore is critical heritage studies since both are mostly concerned with intangible aspects of heritage, and both emphasize ethnographic perspectives, and both are deeply unsatisfied with the status quo of traditional historic preservation practice. Mixing (most) rule-centered historic preservation perspectives with either folklore or critical heritage studies is akin to mixing oil and water, and there is no known homogenizer that will get the two to combine readily. Either we ignore the majority of preservation practice—rooted in laws, rules, and regulations—and focus on the minority aspects of historic preservation that are already compatible with ethnographic perspectives, or we can all work together—via human-centered preservation, folklore, and critical heritage studies—to change practice using social science-based evidence. To be sure, this would require political engagement and advocacy, which is a little-known and potentially risky path, but a path we must accept as fundamental to our shared futures.

Barry Bergey: NEA Folk and Traditional Arts in the U.S.: Infrastructure, Inventory, Impact

[*The following remarks were given at the International Congress on Intangible Cultural Heritage. It was held in Deurne, The Netherlands, February 15-17, 2012, and it was organized by the Dutch Centre for Folk Culture and Intangible Heritage in cooperation with the Fund for Cultural Participation. Over 150 participants, government representatives and policy makers representing the United States, Estonia, Scotland, England, and Flanders attended. Cecile Duvalle, chief of the Intangible Cultural Heritage Section of UNESCO was the keynote speaker.*

One purpose of the meeting, assuming the already in process ratification of the convention by the government, was to guide the Netherlands in the development of an intangible cultural heritage program.]

Introduction

Merv Griffith, a television talk show personality in the United States, is touring Ireland. Upon visiting a pub he noticed a portrait of someone who looked familiar hanging behind the bar. He asked: "Who is that?" The bartender said: "Why that's Joe Heaney, perhaps the greatest Irish singer – he came from here – but now he lives in New York." Merv Griffith thought, *yes and he's the elevator operator and doorman in my apartment building.* Joe Heaney received an National Endowment of the Arts (NEA) National Heritage Fellowship in 1982, the first year that these awards were

53

given.

A stage manager at a large folk festival looks at a performer, an Ethiopian religious song leader, who is about to take the stage. It has just recently been announced that this person will receive an NEA National Heritage Fellowship and the stage manager thinks to himself: *Why, that's the person who tends the parking lot across from the theater where I work.*

Last year, as we assemble the NEA National Heritage Fellows for a group photo in the brand new visitor's center for the U.S. Capitol Building we look up and see on the scaffolding someone etching lettering on an interior cornice. It is Nick Benson, a previous Heritage Fellow from the state of Rhode Island, who was honored two years earlier for carrying on the ancient calligraphy and stone carving techniques handed down in his family.

What kind of program is it, that honors the elevator operators, the parking garage attendants, and the stone carvers for their contributions to the cultural heritage of the United States? What are the keys to success and what are the challenges for such a program recognizing significant achievements in Intangible Cultural Heritage? These are some of the question that I will try to address today. I will speak about three elements that relate to this program – Infrastructure, Inventory, and Impact.

Infrastructure of NEA Folk and Traditional Arts

The NEA is a federal funding agency that supports artistic work in the United States. We are not a cultural ministry, we do not set a national arts policy, but we fund programs such as concerts, exhibitions, media programs, theatrical productions, dance performances, literary work, etc. When the NEA was created in 1965 there was not Folk & Traditional Arts program – the agency was seen as something that then might have been called high culture and major institutions – symphonies, art museums, theater and dance companies – to name just a few. Not until twelve years later was there a stand-alone program at the agency to support the folk arts.

In her first report to the National Council on the Arts, Bess Lomax Hawes, the Folk Arts Director, said: "We have not yet reached the primary goal of both Folk Music and Folk Arts: the recognition and support of the master artists and artisans who embody the multiple aesthetic systems that make life in the United States both so meaningful and so stimulating."

Please note that this statement comes from an activist rather than a preservationist perspective. It emphasized the support of living arts and living artists. It assumed that the major goal of the program should be to present practicing artists and perpetuate the diverse and dynamic living cultural heritage. But how to do it?

In her report Bess outlined three strategies: 1) Support for the direct presentation of folk arts; 2) Support for documentation of the folk arts; and 3) Creating a support system of cultural expertise and institutional stability for the field.

I will address the last of these first – Infrastructure. As she says, "So far, our most successful strategy ... has been to provide partial support for 'folk arts coordinators,' professional folk arts experts who work full time out of a state or local [arts] agency." Folk and community-based artists most frequently work in informal settings with few, if any, institutional support systems. Key to the success of a federal folk arts program was the creation of a network of cultural specialists who could serve as the eyes and ears for a national arts agency, but could also could develop the institutional muscle and skeleton to bring public folk arts programs and projects to fruition. As a result of this early funding, we now have folk arts specialists, most working in state arts agencies or cooperating NGO's, in most of the states in the U.S.

Inventory of NEA Folk and Traditional Arts in the U.S.

As more and more folk arts coordinators were put in place in state, re-gional, and local arts agencies, a second phase of activity began to occur. Cultural specialists began applying for documentation projects – what in the UNESCO Convention on Intangible Cultural Heritage would be called inventories. These statewide surveys allowed the identification of artists and community activities within very particular regions of the country. While identifying endangered cultural practices was not the object of these surveys, ultimately these projects gave cultural specialists the opportunity to gauge the breadth and depth of artistic resources within their region. Because the NEA funds mainly public programs, most of these documenta-tion projects had the long-term goal of producing a festival, an exhibition, or a media product, such as a recording or radio program.

Let me cite just a few of these early efforts in three different regions of the country:

Oregon – A survey that later led to an exhibition entitled "Webfoots and Bunchgrassers: Folk Art of the Oregon Country." The title refers to people of the coast (webfoots) and people of the interior plains (bunchgrassers). The exhibition and catalogue is organized through four framing concepts that both relate to cultural identity and occur roughly in the chronology of the settlement of the region: Native Americans, Pioneers, Buckaroos, and Ethnic Arts. It is worth noting that one of the people featured in the exhibition – Duff Severe, a saddlemaker from Pendleton, OR, was a member of the first group of Heritage recipients in 1982.

Iowa – Moving west to east, a Midwestern state, Iowa, also conducted a survey that resulted in an exhibition, "Passing Time and Traditions: Contemporary Iowa Folk Artists." This exhibition focuses on living artists and views them from the perspective of artistic genres, ethnicity, and geographic location. Its catalogue features the work of Genevieve Mougin, a Lebanese lace worker who received a National Heritage Fellowship in 1984, the third year of the program.

Vermont – Moving to the East, Vermont survey work produced an exhibition entitled "Always in Season: Folk Art and Traditional Culture in Vermont." This exhibition and catalogue focused on material culture and featured both historical and contemporary objects. The organizing principal included three general categories – Native American Heritage, Farmstead and Family Life, and Rural Occupations Off the Farm. Again, a future Heritage Fellow, Newton Washburn, a split ash basketmaker, was featured in this exhibition.

In addition to the fact that each of these surveys and exhibitions featured a future Heritage Fellow, there were several other common characteristics:

1) The documentation and inventory process was carried out by a team of cultural specialists over a period of several years.

2) The exhibitions and the catalogues were rich in explanation and interpretation, featuring labeling and essays that gave cultural and historical context of the items and artists featured.

3) In each case many of the artists identified would be involved in other public programs in subsequent years – festivals, arts in schools activities, master-apprentice programs, media features, etc.

Impact of NEA Folk and Traditional Arts in the U.S.

So far, I've spoken about the building blocks that led to the establishment of the National Endowment for the Arts National Heritage Fellowships program in 1982. The Heritage Fellowship Program honors master folk and traditional artists for their contributions to our nation's living cultural heritage. Anyone can nominate someone for this, the highest form of federal recognition of folk artists. A panel of cultural specialists comes together each year and spends four days reading materials, looking at artistic samples and discussing nominees in order to select around ten artists for this award. The recipients receive $25,000 and come to Washington, DC, to be feted with a ceremony on Capitol Hill, a banquet at the Library of Congress, and a public concert where they perform and demonstrate their art form. To date, we have honored over 350 artists and artistic groups.

What has been the impact? The most obvious, of course, are the various public programs and activities that have resulted from the program. Exhibitions, such as you see here – Films – Concert Series and Festivals featuring the artists – Books – Television and radio programs – Arts in schools curriculum guides – Master/Apprentice programs.

Since we're speaking here of intangible cultural heritage, I thought I might speak a little bit about some of the intangible elements that relate to the Heritage Fellowships, and I will speak of them under three broad categories: Respect, Revitalization, and Return.

Respect

When possible I will try to use the words of the artists themselves. Many folk and traditional artists work quietly within their communities, and sometimes even their neighbors don't recognize their importance to our nation's cultural life. Shining a light on these artists brings national attention to their contributions. This relates to the artist who works as a doorman, who tends a parking garage, or who spends time on the scaffolding working alone — and allows them to emerge from behind the curtain and spend time on the public and political stage.

It also allows the artists, as recipients, to express their respect for tradition and for the elders who taught them. Delores Churchill a Native American weaver of baskets from Alaska, says: "I feel that as a Haida weaver I am just ... passing over and under the warp of my ancestors who are the foundation of this art form.... [My students] will keep the art alive so it continues long after I am gone and no one remembers my name.... This art form belongs to all of us."

Cowboy poet Wally McRae wrote a poem, "My Requiem," that closes thus:

> Some would build an edifice,
> An architectural gem,
> To serve throughout the ages
> As a lasting requiem.
> But grant to me this final wish

> When I say that last amen:
> Let my mark be carved lightly
> In the hearts and minds of men.

Recognition and respect for those intangibles – those things "carved lightly in the hearts and minds of men" – is a great benefit of a program honoring the excellence and contributions of folk and traditional artists.

Revitalization

When Mozell Benson, an African American quilter from Alabama, received her Heritage Fellowship, during the public concert in Washington, DC, the emcee of the program asked if any of her 10 children had taken up quilting. When she answered, "No," Sylvia, her daughter sitting in the audience, said to herself, "Well, that has to change." Her daughter retired from service in the military to return to Alabama and learn from her mother, and today she and her mother teach classes and give workshops for local students.

When Irish dance phenom Michael Flatley came to Washington, DC, to receive his Heritage Fellowship, he had stopped dancing. However, he worked up a little dance program for the concert, and not more than a couple of years later he began to put together the dance program that became Riverdance.

Intangible cultural heritage is a living organic process that needs constant care and attention. Boatmaker Ralph Stanley says: "Building wooden boats is like climbing a still-growing tree where you never get to the top. I keep finding new ways of doing things and new things to do. You can always improve; you're always looking to prove."

Michael Doucet a Cajun fiddler came to Washington, DC, in 1982, the first year of the Heritage Awards, to perform with recipient Dewey Balfa, in his band. Michael formed his own band of younger musicians, and has been responsible for reviving an interest in Cajun music – remaining true to tradition but also taking the music in new and unexpected directions. In 2005 Michael Doucet, himself, came to Washington to receive a National Heritage Fellowship.

This revitalization and renewal feeds the process of living intangible cultural heritage as Ralph Stanley so beautifully put it, "like climbing a still-growing tree."

Return

Finally, as a result of this recognition, recipients most frequently respond with this sense that they need to give back, to return. This usually takes the form of teaching. As Heritage Fellow John Cephas, a blues musician, said to fellow recipients at the Heritage banquet: "It doesn't just stop here. We have another charge. We must try to interest some younger people.... I am dedicated to perpetuating the Blues a long as I have life.... I like to think that the traditional arts hold the world together."

Jean Ritchie, a dulcimer player and singer from the mountainous Appalachian region of the United States, said: "And really, when you think about it, the best immortality anyone can have is that all the generations that come after you still have a little part of you in them."

Many of the Heritage recipients have been recognized for their work teaching the young, and with this honor they continue to participate in Master/Apprentice programs, in school programs, and in community workshops.

In the case of refugee and immigrant artists, this often extends to teaching and starting schools in their country of birth. This has been the case for artists who have come from Cambodia, Viet Nam, India, and Africa.

Conclusion

In conclusion, the National Heritage Fellowships represent one strategy in the efforts to support and sustain folk and traditional arts at the National Endowment for the Arts. This strategy is complemented by granting programs that support the presentation of folk and traditional artists in concerts, exhibitions and media projects and by granting programs that support statewide Master/Apprentice programs and Arts in the Schools programs. All of this is made possible through a viable infrastructure of cultural specialists around the country and an ongoing process of identifying and inventorying the ever-changing cultural assets of our nation's communities, large and small as well as long-standing and newly emerging.

Like climbing the still-growing tree, the Heritage Fellowships are a work in progess, not without their diversions and uncertainties. Because heritage deals with much that is intangible – knowledge, creativity, respect, tradition, responsibility – it is not so easy to measure or define. I think of blacksmiths and ironworkers and Heritage Fellow Francis Whitaker who described looking at an apprentice's work and examining the back side, the side not meant to be seen, in order to determine whether the student took the care to do it right, whether or not the work was meant to be viewed by anyone else. Or I remember the basketmaker Newt Washburn, whose mother told him — when he was making a basket – "Do it right or do it over." I think of the cabinet maker who opens the drawer to look at the quality of the dovetailing to determine the excellence of the work, or the Mennonite quilter who looks at the back of a quilt to see if the stitching is close and consistent. These elements that lie beneath and often are hidden from view are the intangibles that, as John Cephas said, "hold the world together."

The impact of the Fellowships was perhaps best summarized by Bess Lomax Hawes, the person who first conceived of them:

> "Of all the activities assisted by the Folk Arts Program, these fellowships are among the most appreciated and applauded, perhaps because they present to Americans a vision of themselves and of their country, a vision somewhat idealized but profoundly longed for and so, in significant ways, profoundly true. It is a vision of a confident and open-hearted nation, where differences can be seen as exciting instead of fear-laden, where men of good will, across all manner of racial, linguistic, and historical barriers, can find common ground in understanding solid craftsmanship, virtuoso techniques, and deeply felt experiences."

Marti Allen: Heritage Studies and Museums: Supplemental Training for Museum Professionals?

What is the value of heritage studies formal training for museum professionals? Obviously museum professionals are participants in the ever-widening parameters of what constitutes and continues to evolve into heritage studies today. Museum professionals are themselves preservers, promoters, and brokers of heritage through their activities as curators, collections managers, registrars, educators, exhibit techs, fund-raisers, administrators, and so forth. Therefore, why couldn't a museum professional include heritage studies coursework in their curricula, or even replace museum curricula with heritage studies courses? I have been asked to address this question in my capacity of a practicing museum professional who holds a leadership position in a museum and who oversees the hiring of new employees.

Heritage studies curricula are often broad-based and multidisciplinary in approach. Disciplines commonly include those included in this present issue of the *Missouri Folklore Society Journal.* Casting the discipline net wide covers more distance; however, it necessarily limits depth of subject matter. For this reason, heritage studies tend to be heavily theoretic, and students are best poised for pedagogy and placement in academic positions. Curricula will be unlikely to include training in the kind of details and processes that museum professionals need in order to manage collections, monitor loans, and accomplish inventory.

Accordingly, museum professionals who have mastered their jobs and already have training, experience, and accomplishment in everyday museum practices are the best candidates for heritage studies coursework. As a result of taking heritage studies coursework at later points in their careers, accomplished museum professionals report feeling enriched and advantaged by the experience. They may achieve a broader understanding of heritage and new talking points about the value of collections, acquire new insights into interdisciplinary collaboration that advantages themselves and their institution, and strengthen their ability to promote their museums to broader and potentially more lucrative markets. Some achieve advancement or promotions as a result of gaining additional qualifications. Some gain personal satisfaction through broadening their minds, and through advancing opportunities to ruminate about theoretical and idealistic platforms for practice. Perhaps this is why some commentators have (rather crassly) referred to heritage studies degrees as "boutique" degrees.

The situation is entirely different for the student who aspires to work in a museum but has little or no prior training or experience in museums. First, it is imperative for "beginners" to learn about the principal museum disciplines under which positions are categorized, for these are quite different from categories used in heritage studies, and include education, curation, collections management and registration, exhibits, etc. Some museums have more positions; far more museums have only one or two positions, in which case the prospective employee needs expertise in multiple museum disciplines. Very early on, beginners need to explore their interests and aptitudes in some of these disciplines through hands-on opportunities. After one feels sufficiently confident to select a track or a general direction, one must then learn techniques, processes, and guiding principles for best practices in those disciplines. These practices vary according to the kind of museum which houses them: art museum, history or culture museum, natural history museum, zoo, historic house, etc. They also vary according to the subject matters and collection types that each museum specializes in, such as classical art, archaeological materials, cultural resources, plants, live animals, and so forth.

However, there are some things that all museums do, and perhaps the lowest common denominator of functions consists of collections, exhibits, and education. Armed with foundational training and knowledge of practices in these basic disciplines, newly emerging museum professionals will be expected to hit the floor running in the new job, and like as not, in today's harried museum world they will never stop running. From day one of their employment, however, they will start picking up abundant subject knowledge and theory specific to their chosen institution as they fulfill the expectations and requirements of their jobs. They may not have the luxury of choosing what subjects they research or what theories they pick up: these things are likely assigned by management or through need. Real-life museum work affords little room for ruminating; and rarely is pure theory of *anything* put into actual practice. Practitioners use what works for their institution, pulling serviceable aspects from many theories at once. Accordingly, from the perspective of a museum practitioner, I recommend more practice in museum studies curricula, and less theory. Theory specific to the needs of an institution will come as employees mature in the job and have time to expand their horizons.

Therefore, substituting a heritage studies regime for a museum studies regime in the case of those who have little or no prior museum training or experience would not constitute the preferred preparation for museum employment. When it comes to museum leadership, likewise, the advantaged candidate will have a solid foundation in museum disciplines and a thorough understanding of—and at least some experience in—the practice s/he will be expected to oversee. Those who are already accomplished in museum practices could potentially enhance their candidacy for promotion or leadership positions by supplementing their training with coursework or a degree in heritage studies. For students entering a heritage studies program with no museum background but aspiring to include museum employment as a possible career, special advising is imperative. Indeed, what is probably most needed in a heritage studies curriculum in these cases, is a good dose of training in museum practices. What paperwork is needed to properly accept donations and monitor loans and otherwise keep your institution legally safe? How do you develop and assess learning outcomes for educational programs, or write lesson plans compliant with state-mandated curriculum? Rather than duplicate what museum studies programs are doing already, it may be more efficient to allow the beginning museum-aspiring heritage studies student to substitute a good museum practices course or an internship for other required classes.

Ruth Hawkins: Putting Principles into Practice: Cultural Heritage Tourism Challenges

Just over 20 years ago, Arkansas State University in Jonesboro accidentally became involved in cultural heritage tourism. At that time, our Institutional Advancement office and various faculty members were assisting mayors, county judges, and other community leaders and residents in an effort to establish a route through an eight-county area in Eastern Arkansas as a National Scenic Byway. In the process of doing the required analysis of intrinsic qualities along the route (natural, cultural, archeological, historic, recreational, and scenic), we realized there was no strong anchor attraction at the north end of the route (established in 1998 as Crowley's Ridge Parkway National Scenic Byway).

The assessment also highlighted that at one time Ernest Hemingway spent a lot of time in Piggott (the northernmost town of any size along the route) at the home of his in-laws, Paul and Mary Pfeiffer. Hemingway was married to their daughter, Pauline Pfeiffer, from 1927-1940, and made periodic trips from Key West to visit her family and write. In fact, portions of *A Farewell to Arms*, along with several short stories, were written in a barn that the Pfeiffers converted for his use as a studio. We soon learned that not only did this property still exist, but it was for sale. Taking that as a sign, we knew we needed to move quickly, lest a private buyer acquire the barn studio and either tear it down or continue its private use, thus removing the possibility of it becoming a cultural heritage attraction.

With no long-term organization in place for the Byways group to acquire the property, Arkansas State University stepped in, with the help of grants and a legislative appropriation, and became the owner of what developed into the Hemingway-Pfeiffer Museum and Educational Center. In the beginning, we had no hands-on experience or expertise in preservation, tourism, or cultural heritage, but we did hire a consultant with restoration experience through Main Street America, a subsidiary of the National Trust for Historic Preservation.

Much of what we did in that first preservation project was intuitive, later validated when we established a Heritage Studies Ph.D. program in 2001. By then we had already established the Arkansas Heritage Sites program, which operates independently from the academic program but serves as a field school and research laboratory for many of the Ph.D. courses and graduate assistantships. Theories and principles explored through the degree program provided a cultural heritage framework and guideposts for our future projects, which also include the Southern Tenant Farmers Museum in Tyronza, the Lakeport Plantation near Lake Village, the Rohwer Japanese American Relocation Center, and the Historic Dyess Colony: Johnny Cash Boyhood Home. At each of these sites we faced different challenges that we approached in various ways. In some cases we succeeded; in others we are still working at it.

Without consciously focusing on these guidelines at the time, our work essentially followed five key principles[1] espoused by the National Trust for Historic Preservation, a longtime leader in the study and promotion of cultural heritage tourism:

- **Collaboration**

  In our case, we were already working with a broad group on the Byways project, but we had to get additional buy-in and support from each of the communities where our projects are located. Because some of these projects dealt with controversial subjects, inclusiveness was critical to ensure that all viewpoints were represented.

- **Find the Fit Between the Community and Tourism**

  At some of our sites, aspects of the community's heritage was not pretty. Working within these communities, we found that people often did not know aspects of their heritage, or they had forgotten or did not want to remember. Though we never faced outright hostility, there were detractors who did not want to open old wounds, or who simply didn't see or believe that their community had something of interest to outside visitors.

---

[1]National Trust for Historic Preservation, "Principles of Successful Heritage Tourism," *Partnering to Promote Heritage Tourism in Local Communities: Guidance for Federal Agencies*, http://www.achp.gov/ht/principles.html. Last Updated March 3, 2006.

- **Make Sites and Programs Come Alive**

  As a university, it was critical to us that thorough research be done on each site, and how it functioned historically, so that we could tell nationally important stories accurately and in ways that would capture the attention and interests of visitors.

- **Focus on Quality and Authenticity**

  This was the cornerstone of all of our projects from the beginning. We did not start on restoration/preservation at any of our sites, or begin to develop interpretation, until we researched how the site was lived in or utilized, and how it appeared architecturally during the period of significance.

- **Preserve and Protect**

  Best practices according to Secretary of Interior Standards for the Treatment of Historic Properties often had to be balanced with financial resources, but in no cases did we make important decisions that weren't reversible. This continues to be a concern in some cases where visitor traffic can lead to degradation of significant cultural resources.

Given the above, in the remainder of this article I will attempt to point out some of the major challenges that we faced at each site. It is by no means an exhaustive case study of each (that would require a series of separate articles), but I want to highlight some of the issues involved in putting principles into practice.

Hemingway-Pfeiffer Museum and Educational Center

This site, which opened in 1999, consists of the Pfeiffers' home, the barn studio they adapted for Ernest Hemingway's use, a smaller residence used as an educational center, expansive grounds, and the former school property across the street which has yet to be developed. Along with their association with Ernest Hemingway, the Pfeiffer family was important in their own right. Formerly a partner with his brothers in Pfeiffer Pharmaceuticals in St. Louis, Paul Pfeiffer moved his family to Piggott in 1913, ultimately owning 63,000 acres of land in the area. He rented the land to tenant farmers, later selling it to them on reasonable financial terms, and was responsible for many improvements in the community, including serving as bank president in order to keep the bank open during the Great Depression. Their daughter Pauline was in one of the early graduating classes at the University of Missouri School of Journalism. After working as a writer for a time in New York, she was with *Vogue* magazine in Paris when she met Hemingway and his wife, later becoming Wife No. 2.

Though this was our first heritage site, we made some decisions that have served us well throughout all of our projects. First and foremost, during the restoration we determined that we would not lift a hammer or a paint brush until what we were doing could be verified by at least three sources. For example, to determine the paint color on the walls during the time that Hemingway was there (late '20s and early '30s), we (1) sent core paint samples to a laboratory to analyze the makeup and coloration of each layer, starting from when the house was built and proceeding through time; (2) conducted oral histories with housekeepers and family members who were there during the Hemingway era to determine what they remembered about wall colors; and (3) used visual inspection, such as finding paint behind floor radiators that were installed in the mid-1930s, thus never being painted afterward and retaining the color that existed before that time.

Major Challenges to Overcome

- **Belief that Hemingway hated Piggott—and Piggott hated Hemingway!**

  Many people could not understand why we wanted to do anything related to Ernest Hemingway in the community, as they did not think much of him, and the feeling seemed to have been mutual. This last assumption was based on various biographers who picked up on a comment in a personal letter that Hemingway wrote to his editor. After arriving in Piggott for his first visit, he wrote "Am now at the above address – a christ offal place."[2] In truth, Hemingway arrived during an unseasonable heat wave that caused even Mary Pfeiffer, his saintly mother-in-law, to complain. Though this off-handed remark became the accepted characterization of Hemingway's views of Piggott, few of its residents ever read or remembered a quote from Hemingway's "Paris Letter," which appeared in a 1934 issue of *Esquire* magazine. In that article, he wrote "Paris was . . . a fine place to be quite young in . . . now I much prefer life out on the ranch,

[2]Ernest Hemingway letter to Maxwell Perkins, May 31, 1928, Princeton University Library. Also in Carlos Baker, Ed., *Ernest Hemingway: Selected Letters 1917-1961* (New York: Charles Scribner's Sons, 1981), 278.

or in Piggott, Arkansas, in the fall . . ."[3] Similarly, in a letter to Mary Pfeiffer, Hemingway noted, "I like the house in Piggott much better than the White House. . . . Am glad to have met them [the Roosevelts] but wouldn't care to live there."[4]

- **Belief that Hemingway never spent much time in Piggott**

    A common criticism from outside the community questioned why we would create a museum focused heavily on Ernest Hemingway when he never spent that much time in Piggott, or even in Arkansas. Counteracting this view took lots of research, primarily into all of Hemingway's letters to friends postmarked from Piggott, as well as letters to the Pfeiffers discussing upcoming trips or commenting on completed trips. To document this in a very visible way, we created a timeline that stretches across one wall of the barn studio. Each year of the timeline contains 12 small rectangles, representing months in the year, with the rectangles filled in for the months Heming- way was actually in Piggott. The timeline also includes information about specific visits, photos from each year, and quotes pulled from correspondence with the Pfeiffers.

- **Keeping it Exciting– Constant Challenge**

    Since this site is primarily a house museum, it is difficult to keep it interesting for returning visitors. We attempt to have temporary exhibits and special events to show off various aspects of the site, but lack of appropriate space limits what we can do. Much of our success with repeat visitors comes from educational programming, such as adult writers' retreats, veterans' retreats, readers' retreats, after-school writing programs for students, and special tours.

Southern Tenant Farmers Museum

This site is located in the historic Mitchell-East Building, which once housed H. L. Mitchell's dry cleaning establishment on one side and Clay East's service station on the other. Mitchell and East, both Socialists, were concerned about the unfair practices of many landlords during the Great Depression. Upon advice from Norman Thomas, national Socialist candi- date for president, they provided leadership for organizing the Southern Tenant Farmers Union in 1934. It was the first agricultural union in the

---

[3] Ernest Hemingway, "Paris Letter," *Esquire* (February 1934), 22.

[4] Ernest Hemingway letter to Mary Pfeiffer, Aug. 2,, 1937, Princeton University Library. Also in Baker, *Selected Letters*, 460-461.

country to involve both black and white farmers in the same union, integrated down through the local chapter level, as well as to place many women in leadership positions.

The Mitchell-East Building served as informal union headquarters until threats of violence forced relocation across the river to Memphis. The building, which opened in 2006, has been restored to its original appearance on the exterior, including recreating the original signage, the early Lion Gas Station pumps, and promotional lettering on the windows. Exhibits inside the building, primarily photographic, trace the history of tenant farming in Northeast Arkansas, as well as the rise and fall of the Union. A former bank building next door also was renovated as a reception area, offices, and gift shop.

An initial problem at this site was the fact that chemicals had leeched into the soil while the gas station was operating, along with other environmental issues, making it a brownfield site. Early activities in this project focused on these concerns, including working closely with the Arkansas Department of Environmental Quality.

Major Challenges to Overcome

• Landowners Wanted this Chapter in History Buried

Some of the leaders in the community saw no point in dredging up the past, believing that it would serve only to create new rifts between landowners and renters. Additionally, there was a fear that the heritage site would present just one side of the story. For example, there were many cases of landlords evicting sharecroppers to avoid giving them their share of government subsidies enacted as a relief measure. But there were other cases where sharecroppers left in the middle of the night, legitimately owing money to their landlords for items purchased on credit. Others believed that many of the Union activities, such as the 1939 Sharecroppers Strike in the Missouri Bootheel, were the result of outside agitators. Many of these concerns among present-day landowners disappeared after the museum opened, and they saw that it was as much a story about tenant farming and sharecropping in the 1930s, as it was about the Union and its activities. Today, many of these early naysayers bring visitors to the museum.

• Former Union Members Feared Retaliation

While the Union membership swelled during the late 1930s to some 30,000 farmers across the south, finding any of those members to talk about it today was difficult. Most who actually farmed during the 1930s were deceased, while their children either had been protected from knowing about their parents' Union activities, or they remained reluctant to talk about them. Thus, much of our information about the Union came from books, articles, and speeches by its leadership, as well as from the official papers of the Southern Tenant Farmers Union (including letters from individual tenants and sharecroppers seeking redress of grievances). We continue to strive to identify people with connections to the Union or to tenant farming in the region, and we keep videotaping equipment set up in a small room in case a visitor drops in with a story to tell.

- **"You are putting two Socialists on a pedestal."**

Some landowners in the community insisted that Mitchell and East did not really care about the plight of tenant farmers and sharecroppers. There was concern that these two men were being glorified for their actions, when in reality all they were interested in was recruiting people to the Socialist party. Others had additional negative views about the two men, suggesting that their motives were not pure. Even if some of the accusations were true, tenant farmers and sharecroppers joined the Union in an effort to feed their families, so it is highly unlikely that they cared much about anyone's political affiliations. Concern about focusing on Mitchell and East was assuaged only after we opened and people were able to see that they were only a small part of the story.

Lakeport Plantation

Arkansas State University acquired the Lakeport Plantation near Lake Village in 2001 and opened it to the public in 2007, after extensive restoration utilizing Department of Interior best practices. This house is significant for several reasons:

- It is Arkansas's last plantation home on the Mississippi River.

- It retains most of its original architectural features and finishes, including wood graining on the doors and faux marble graining on the fireplace mantels.

- It tells the story of the politically prominent Johnson family that included a vice president of the United State, governors, congressmen, federal judges, and others who migrated from Virginia to Kentucky to Mississippi and Arkansas.

• The land has remained in continuous cotton production since the 1830s, thus documenting black agricultural experiences at Lakeport. This included clearing the land and converting it to agricultural production, remaining on the plantation during the Civil War, becoming tenant farmers after the war, migrating to the north when agriculture became mechanized, and now returning to the region.

Major Challenges to Overcome

• Involvement of the Black Community

This was by far our biggest challenge and remains an issue. We erroneously assumed that the black community would be interested in helping to restore and interpret the house because we had documented evidence that the house was built almost entirely by enslaved labor. Instead, we found that very few black residents descended directly from enslaved laborers at Lakeport, and they saw very few connections with the "Big House." Instead, their memories focused on experiences as tenant farmers living in the "quarters" near the house, and they wanted to see one or more of the these houses rebuilt to tell their stories. Because the former quarters location is now a privately owned cotton field, we did not have the ability to follow through on this. Instead, we gathered oral histories from many of the former tenant farmers and placed excerpts on a kiosk in a room of the house that looks out toward where the quarters once were. We also incorporated interpretation throughout the house related to enslaved laborers as well as to later tenant farmers at Lakeport. Additionally, because the commissary attached to the house was the only room black residents connected with, we furnished it the way they remembered it from the 1930s. Nevertheless, their view remains that their ancestors were not slaves there, and it is not part of their heritage.

• Lead Paint Abatement

There were numerous challenges with the actual restoration, but perhaps the most difficult was dealing with a decision by environmental experts that all paint, including the original finishes, had to be stripped from the house due to lead paint issues. There was a major standoff, and work shut down for several weeks while we documented how the abatement could be handled without removing the original finishes. It was resolved only when we agreed to essentially shrink-wrap the entire house, with HEPA filters spaced sporadically to keep lead particles at acceptable levels. One section of the wrap at a time was opened for lead paint removal and encapsulation of historic finishes.

- **How to Interpret the House**

During the process of restoration, we put together a team of experts from across the state, including historians, archeologists, architects, historic finish specialists, restoration specialists, and others. There was deep division among the team as to how the house should be interpreted. Some wanted to completely furnish the house as it would have looked in its heyday (even though we had very little of the original furniture). Others wanted to leave the house completely empty, so the architecture and the skilled craftsmanship evident throughout the house could speak for themselves. Ultimately, we made a decision that has been a big plus for the house. For the first five years we left the house completely empty, devoid of any exhibits. As visitors toured the house, we made notes of the kinds of questions they asked and what aspects they appeared to be interested in. We then developed our interpretation based on this visitor input and instructed our exhibit designers that the house itself must remain the major exhibit, with nothing hanging on the walls or obstructing architectural features. The result is a series of free-standing translucent panels and interactive kiosks strategically placed throughout the house, along with ambient sounds from inside and outside the house.

Rohwer Japanese American Relocation Center

After the bombing of Pearl Harbor during WWII, thousands of Japanese Americans, mostly from the West Coast, were rounded up and put into internment camps out of fear that they would assist the enemy. This was despite the fact that almost two-thirds were American citizens. Ten internment camps were established, primarily in western states, but two were placed in Arkansas — at Rohwer and at Jerome. Little is left of the Jerome camp other than a smokestack; and a hospital smokestack and a cemetery remain at Rohwer. Arkansas State University was asked in 2010 to consider interpretation for Rohwer that could be placed near the cemetery. After extensive research and planning, eight audio panels were installed in 2013. Each exhibit contains an audio button with narratives from actor

George Takei, who was interned with his family at Rohwer at age five.[5]

Major Challenges to Overcome

- ### Lingering Issues and Old Wounds

  For many years after WWII there was sentiment against Japanese Americans, even though most were U. S. citizens, because they happened to look like the enemy. It is perhaps only in recent years that people in the region have been supportive of commemorating the sacrifices of Japanese Americans during the war. Additionally, in the segregated south during WWII, there were many citizens who faced racial discrimination and/or went without adequate food, clothing, and shelter. Thus, there often was resentment that the people inside the fence, even though they were being held against their will, were being treated far better than some of the residents outside the camp.

- ### Adequate Input from Japanese Americans

  Developing the exhibits required major and ongoing input from Japanese American stakeholders — a challenge because only one family from Rohwer remains in Arkansas. Many interned in this camp or other camps are still living, however, and their experiences were important to capture and understand. Even differences in terminology had to be understood and weighed. For example, official government terms for these sites were internment camps or relocation centers. But to Japanese Americans, they met the true definition of concentration camps. It was critical to the success of our project that all exhibit copy was read and commented on by members of several Japanese American groups around the country.

- ### Confusion with Prisoners of War

  In talking with others and seeking support for the Rohwer Japanese American Relocation Center, the immediate response of many is "Oh, our town had a similar prisoner of war camp for Germans." Or for Italians. We constantly must point out that these Japanese American camps were different. These were not prisoners of war. These were men, women, and children – mostly U. S. citizens – whose only "war crime" was that they happened to look like the enemy. This is a huge difference.

---

[5]For updates on the Rohwer Heritage see "Rohwer Reconstructed: Interpreting Place Through Experience" https://risingabove.cast.uark.edu/home and the Chikaraishi article in this journal.

Historic Dyess Colony: Johnny Cash Boyhood Home

Arkansas State University opened the Historic Dyess Colony: Johnny Cash Boyhood Home in April 2014 as our latest heritage site. Beyond its most famous resident, Dyess also is nationally significant as one of the oldest, and by far the largest, agricultural resettlement colonies created during the New Deal. Through this program, the federal government selected 500 out-of-work farm families, from every county in Arkansas, and relocated them to twenty and forth-acre farmsteads. The Cash family from Cleveland County, including three-year-old J. R. Cash, was among the chosen ones. When Eleanor Roosevelt came to inspect in 1936, two years after its establishment, the colony was at its peak of about 3,000 people.

Today, Dyess is an incorporated town with only 415 residents and very little visitor infrastructure. The former colony Administration Building has been restored; it now houses exhibits related to the establishment of the colony, everyday life in the colony, and the impact of growing up in Dyess on Johnny Cash and his music. A Visitors Center with a gift shop, auditorium, offices, and other exhibit space is next door in the re-created Dyess Theatre and Pop Shop. Finally, the Johnny Cash Boyhood Home — located on a gravel road about 1.5 miles from the colony center — has been restored and furnished as it looked when the Cash family lived there, based on memories of his two living siblings, Joanne Cash Yates and Tommy Cash.

Major Challenges to Overcome

- **Protecting our Greatest Assets**

   Preserving and protecting the Cash home is our most daunting challenge. This is a small house, and the thousands of visitors walking through each year are taking their toll. For example, from the beginning we required visitors to slip booties over their shoes to avoid damage to the original linoleum on the living room floor. Even so, we are beginning to have significant damage and are now considering making a duplicate of the floor covering and storing the original. We will continue to face such challenges throughout the home.

- **Balance between the Dyess Colony Story and the Johnny Cash Story**

   People from Dyess take pride in Johnny Cash and recognize that he is what draws visitors to the community. But they also hope that guests leave understanding the strong role that the agricultural resettlement colony played in shaping Cash's values, as well as the impact that it had on all their lives. We are sensitive to this and attempt to weave the two stories together as much as possible. For example, the Johnny Cash home is one of only a handful of colony houses that still exist and, thus, is representative of how every colonist family lived in Dyess. Cash's childhood stories and memories are much the same as the memories of every Dyess colonist. In a letter to his first wife, Vivian, before they married, he wrote of Dyess, "Every tree, stump, bush or every square foot of that place has a memory for me. . . . Every inch . . . makes me think of something different, something wonderful and precious that happened."[6] We try to weave these strong connections between Cash, the land, and the Dyess Colony into all of our interpretations.

- **Common Ground between Historic Agriculture and Modern Farming Practices**

When Dyess was an agricultural resettlement community, farmsteads consisted of twenty to forty acres, planted mostly in cotton. Today, very little cotton is grown, as crops such as soybeans, corn, and rice have become more profitable. And rather than forty acres, it is more likely that a farm has 640 acres (a section). Though the town remains rural, giving visitors a glimpse into what life was like in the 1930s and 1940s is difficult. Modern farming practices present issues to think about where tourists are concerned. For example, widespread use of chemicals and pesticides in surrounding fields can lead to poor air quality. Special events at the house can be impacted by the noise of low-flying crop dusters or by farmers plowing adjacent fields and stirring up dust. Thus, it is essential to coordinate with farmers so that they know what events we have coming up and can work with us. In some cases, we have had to be creative, such as planting rows of cotton to form the perimeter of the field where the Johnny Cash Heritage Festival takes place. Thus, people who have never seen cotton can grab a few bolls as they leave.

- **Lack of Infrastructure**

This is a major problem for the ongoing success of this heritage site. The town of Dyess has one gas station/general store and one car-wash. There are no restaurants other than basic sandwiches at the

---

[6] John R. Cash Letter to Vivian Liberto, November 23, 1953, Cash Daughters Private Collection.

general store. There is no lodging within twenty miles, and no retail shop for tourists. In addition, the town has drainage problems causing ditches to overflow; and a number of run-down houses need to be demolished. If we are truly going to promote Johnny Cash as a product of the Dyess Colony, the entire town must become an integral part of the heritage tourism site. In particular, this includes enforcing ordinances, addressing drainage and paving issues, and seeking out entrepreneurs who can develop the much-needed visitor amenities.

The challenges cited above for Arkansas State's heritage sites are simply a means of pointing out that putting the five National Trust principles into practice can take heritage professionals in multiple and often unexpected directions. Flexibility and patience must be part of the heritage professional's tool kit.

A Pictorial Commemoration of Ruth Hawkins' Heritage Contributions (Photos by Gregory Hansen)

Hemingway-Pfeiffer Museum and Educational Center

Ernest Hemingway Barn Studio, Piggott, Arkansas,
Listed on the National Register of Historic Places, 1982

Interior of Hemingway's Barn Studio
(recreated and imagined from A-State collection)

Southern Tenant Farmers Museum

Southern Tenant Farmers Museum,
Mural by Connie Watkins

Southern Tenant Farmers Museum,
Site Listed on National Register of Historic Places in 2010

Gas Station Operated by Union Organizer, Clay East
at the Southern Tenant Farmers Museum

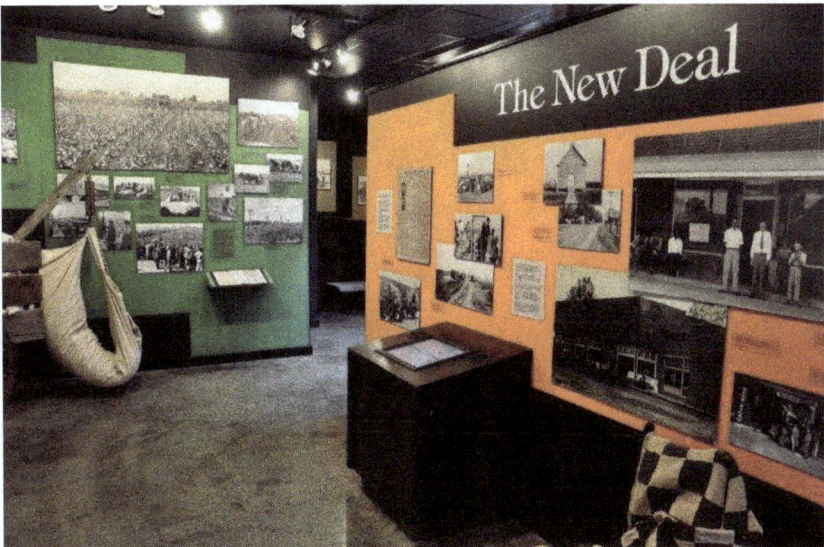

Interior of Southern Tenant Farmers Museum, Tyronza, Arkansas

Lakeport Plantation

Lakeport Plantation, Lake Village, Arkansas
House Listed on National Register of Historic Places in 1974

Replication of the Commissary, Lakeport Plantation

Stairway at Lakeport Plantation Home,
Built in 1859 by Slaves Owned by Lycurgus and Lydia Johnson

Historic Dyess Colony: Johnny Cash Boyhood Home

Façade of Dyess Theatre with Original Projector
Photo made on 8/16/2014, Opening Day of Historic Dyess Colony

Johnny Cash Boyhood Home, 8/16/2014,
Listed on the National Register of Historic Places, 2018

Cash Family Piano, Dyess

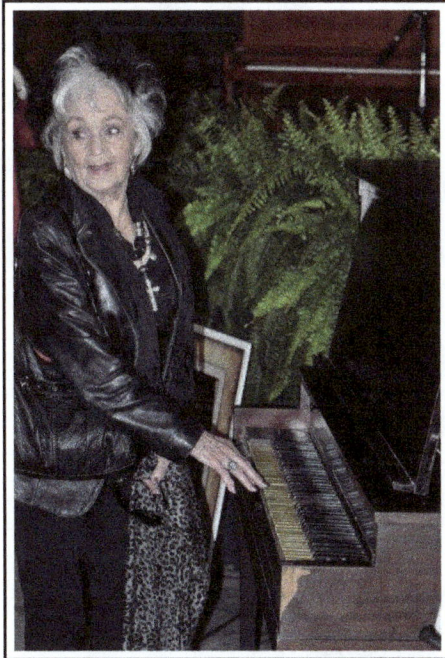

Joanne Cash Yates at the family piano, 2/26/2012, Dyess

Nancy Chikaraishi: "Life Interrupted": A Visual Heritage Study

"Life Interrupted: Art for Social Change" is a series of art and cultural events exploring the Japanese-American Internment Camps of World War II. In February 2017, the Drury University events in Springfield, Missouri, included a roundtable discussion with local multicultural leaders, a First Friday Art Walk installation, a dance workshop and story circle, and a professional dance performance by the renowned CORE Performance Company of Houston and Atlanta.

These richly-layered events draw from my own heritage: my parents and grandparents were interned in Rohwer, Arkansas in 1942. The layers expressing this heritage developed over time—first with charcoal sketches, then with events at the Rohwer Heritage Site, then with lectures and presentations, more art work, sculptures, music and dance. Collaborations involving many disciplines and individuals made it possible for those who did not experience the internments as a personal heritage to recognize them as part of a broader American heritage. While rooted in a particular and painful Japanese American story, the work which now constitutes "Life Interrupted" seeks to convey a universality of experience with deep resonance for contemporary issues such as postwar emigration, and the xenophobia that erupts in response. Seventy-seven years after Executive Order 9066 authorized the Internment Camps, "Life Interrupted" asks how issues of civil rights violations, racial profiling, discrimination and immigration have shifted, changed, or remained constant.

How do we ensure the safety of our country without discriminating against ethnicity, religion or gender? What are some solutions to change behaviors, values, and actions, to create a safer, more tolerant and peaceful world? How can we learn from this troubling part of our American heritage? Seventy-seven years after FDR's Order interrupted the lives of 110,000 people, where are we on these issues?

Camps Rising Out of the Fields

I visited the rural site of the Rohwer Arkansas Internment camp where my parents both were interned. This swampy land near the Mississippi River was drained for the camps. As I stood and walked among the acres of cotton fields, I could imagine the camps rising out of the fields.

The Internment Camps (plywood, wire, wire mesh, spray paint)

This sculpture represents the population in each of the 10 internment camps. The strings of cots above each box represent the number of people in that camp at a ratio of 1:500. Each cot represents 500 persons. The population of each camp is shown in orange in the bottom of each box. The lives of 120,000 Japanese aliens and Japanese Americans were abruptly interrupted and suspended due to war hysteria.

Life in Limbo 9' x 40' x 9'

The suspended rock sculpture represents the chaos, confusion and uncertainty in the suspended lives of the internees imprisoned in the camps. Where were they going? What would life be like? What will the future bring? Today, aliens seeking asylum, children in detention centers and those with DACA status are also in this state of limbo.

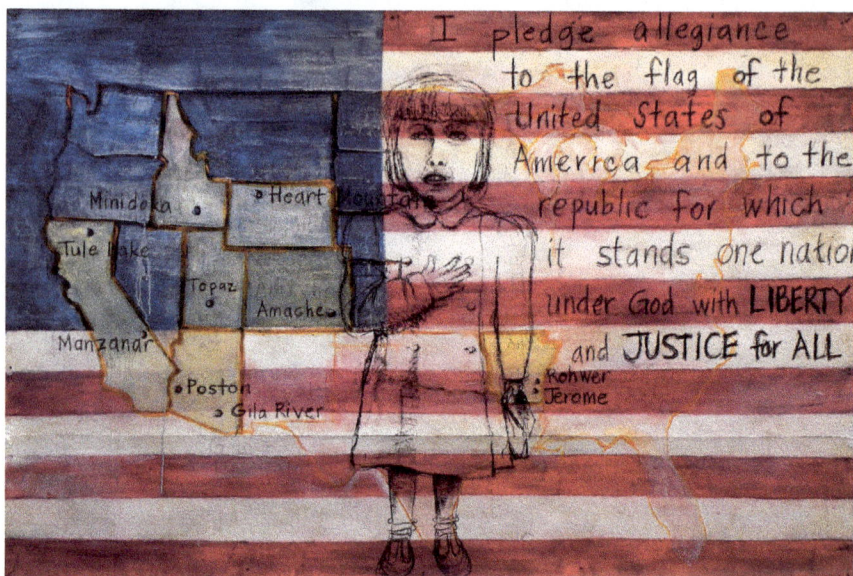

Liberty and Justice for All

In the camps, children recited the pledge of allegiance in school. The phrase "liberty and justice for all" is ironic as these children and their families were held behind barbed wire fences.

My Father's Story
The story is told in the image, which is part of the exhibit's timeline.

Natalie M. Underberg-Goode: Digital Heritage

I have used the critical heritage discourse and, more broadly, heritage studies in my work in several ways. My research examines the use of digital media to preserve and disseminate folklore and cultural heritage, with a focus on digital storytelling and participatory new media design and practice. As a folklorist by training who teaches and conducts research in the field of digital media, I seek to build productive conceptual bridges between heritage and digital media professionals and scholars. This certainly relates to current discussions about the digitization of cultural heritage, and the growing concern to safeguard intangible cultural heritage (hereafter ICH) through digital media, and to disseminate it. I am also increasingly interested in how we can integrate insights from participatory design methodology into digital heritage work.

Heritage studies also relates to my work in the sense of trying to represent complex issues related to ICH such as representing social experience, or how our social position or perspective may affect the way we experience and understand ICH. As heritage scholars have pointed out, it is important to consider how different individuals and communities may understand and relate to ICH depending upon their perspective. Heritage scholars (such as Basu and Zetterstrom-Sharp, 2015; Ruggles and Sinha, 2009; Solomon and Peters, 2009) point out the way that insiders and outsiders (broadly defined) may hold differing and, at times, conflicting ways of interpreting the meaning, function, and value of ICH.

So, in my work, I try to use digital media's ability to support character (Alexander 2011) and to represent diverse perspectives or points of view to convey the diversity of perspectives on social experience. For example,

PeruDigital, a Website project that shares and interprets Peruvian festivals and related folklore, based on the archives of the Institute of Ethnomusicology at the Pontifical Catholic University of Peru, cues visitors to this approach beginning in the first environment in which the user lands, the Plaza Francia in Lima, Peru, where the visitor can meet the ethnography student character who will accompany him/her throughout the site. In addition, the visitor will encounter a woman playing the guitar from the North Coast who serves as a lead-in to the focus on performance in the festival environment encountered later in the exploration of the Website.

More recently, in the Portal to Peru project, based on the photographic archives of and interviews I have conducted with members of the Center for Traditional Textiles in Cusco, Peru, the interactive environment section of the Website project presents three storylines through which the user can role-play as different social actors. Visitors are invited to step into the shoes of a volunteer, tourist, or weaving student. Here visitors can first view digital stories about the personal experiences of women who work with the Center for Traditional Textiles (CTTC), before exploring interactive visual novels that help relate the weavings created by Center members to broader themes that affect their lives such as tourism, globalization, and preservation of cultural heritage.

In the volunteer perspective, the interactor visits Nilda Callañaupa, the CTTC director, at her office to learn more about volunteering with the Center, as well as the way they function as a business. In the weaver perspective, the player visits Susana (one of the weavers who I interviewed) in Piturmarca — one of the ten communities with whom the CTTC works — to learn more about the community culture, and the process of weaving, from shearing to completion. Or the visitor can adopt the tourist perspective through visiting Rosita (a sales associate who I interviewed) at the CTTC store to learn more about fair trade, textile quality, and the importance behind textile techniques and designs.

Another way that I use heritage studies in my work is to focus on ways to share with audiences cultural values and ideas about time, space, or movement, or, more abstract aspects of ICH that may be challenging to explain to others. Cultural heritage is not only communicated through customs, material culture, and other visible forms, but also through key cultural ideas, whether about the cosmos, relations between humans, relations with nature, the nature of time, or something else.

So, in my work, I try to leverage the expressive potential of new media, its ability to create immersive, interactive or navigable spaces, and its ability to enable multilinear story presentation formats to allow for design and navigation choices that simulate in certain ways aspects of cultural experience. So, for example, in the PeruDigital project, navigation is structured through types of questions a visitor would need to ask, information a visitor would need to know, or things a visitor would need to be able to do. A key Peruvian cultural concept (like wealth as expressed through the ability to mobilize cooperative labor) can be explored by the visitor by following the festival coordinator or sponsor's path (presented as moving toward a goal — for example to help organize the festival — and as a set of questions the user is encouraged to find answers to by combining Website exploration and personal reflection). In the more recent project Portal to Peru, Andean aesthetic preferences for bright colors, in particular the preference for red and green, are given design prominence in the graphic design of the site itself. Explanations for the preference, and the role such a color aesthetic plays, are embedded in the weavers' negotiations with tourists and in larger market explorations.

Critical heritage work offers both benefits and challenges to scholars and practitioners. As critical heritage studies involves considering the power dynamics of how we define and share "heritage," we know that increasing opportunities for people to participate in heritage discourse and practice is important. The 2003 Convention on ICH explicitly encourages communities to play a role in defining, preserving, and disseminating heritage. Increasingly, too, digital heritage practitioners seek to involve community members and other stakeholders in the design and production of heritage projects in a way that seeks to break down barriers between the scholar and the communities they represent. This represents both a benefit and, at times, a challenge, as those involved in the heritage field well know (Aria, Christofano, and Maltese 2015; Van Hout 2015).

The work I do in digital heritage typically adopts a collaborative approach, inspired by insights from participatory research and design (Gubrium and Harper 2013). In this approach, the ethnographer or folklorist seeks to work with individuals and communities to devise cultural representations that reflect the way they would like to be represented, if they had the access to resources, design experience, or technical expertise which the heritage studies professional has. For example, with the Portal to Peru project, the Website design and interpretive approach (including the visual novel's interactive narratives) were determined and refined through an ongoing dialogue with members of the Center for Traditional Textiles, including both in-person (while I was in Cusco) and virtual (via Skype) sessions. This allowed us to identify key themes and concerns the Website should be designed to address, such as the importance of helping tourists understand the difference between high and low quality textiles, and the rationale for the difference in cost between textiles which Center members sell and those that could be found across the street at a non-fair-trade market. The opportunity to open up the so-called "black box" of digital media design and production is an important skill that digital heritage practitioners can and should add to their toolset.

More broadly, I think we each bring with us some central ideas from within our own academic discipline(s) that could make a contribution to the heritage discourse. From folkloristics, a focus on living cultural heritage and the people who create and perform it is one that I bring to my work. Because traditions are always changing, I think there is value in a focus on the people performing the intangible cultural heritage. Field recordings and archive materials, while capturing valuable information for future use and appreciation, can also serve to decontextualize that same heritage, separating it from its original performance context. Digital design choices that allow users to adopt a social role and see the same story/artifact from multiple perspectives can help to re-contextualize that heritage "object" and help audiences better understand the traditional skills and knowledge, as well as the broader social contexts that make those heritage performances and objects possible.

Going forward, there are certainly multiple urgent questions that heritage studies/critical heritage studies in the context of the US need to address. In terms of digital heritage, I really think long-term preservation issues are critical, including technological obsolescene and institutional (or, more precisely, project management) memory. We need to be prepared to port projects from one platform to another, and to design with the long view in mind. This includes documenting the institutional knowledge necessary to create digital heritage projects (Cameron and Robinson 2007). That is why in my scholarship I seek to open up the design and development process — to make that "black box of development" less opaque. The focus on process in my work extends beyond the processes of ICH to the processes of interpreting and presenting ICH through digital media.

References

Alexander, B. (2017). *The New digital storytelling: Creating narratives with new media–revised and updated edition.* ABC-CLIO.

Aria, M., Cristofano, M. and Maltese, S. (2015). Development challenges and shared heritage-making processes in Southwest Ghana." In Paul Basu and Wayne Modest (Eds.) *Museums, heritage and international development* (pp. 150-169). Routledge.

Basu, P. and Zetterstrom-Sharp, J. (2015). Complicating culture for development: Negotiating 'dysfunctional heritage'in Sierra Leone. In

Paul Basu and Wayne Modest (Eds.) *Museums, heritage and international development* (pp. 61-92). Routledge.

Cameron, F. and Robinson, H. (2007). Digital knowledgescapes: Cultural, theoretical, practical, and usage issues facing museum collection databases in a digital epoch.In Fiona Cameron and Sarah Kenderdine (Eds.) *Theorizing digital cultural heritage: A critical discourse* (pp.165-191). MIT Press.

Gubrium, A. and Harper, K. (2013).*Participatory visual and digital methods* (Vol 10. Developing Qualitative Inquiry Series). Routledge.

Ruggles, D.F. and Sinha, A. (2009). Preserving the cultural landscape heritage of Champaner-Pavagadh, Gujarat, India. In D.F. Ruggles and H. Silverman (Eds.) *Intangible Heritage Embodied* (pp. 79-99). New York: Springer.

Salomon, F. and Peters, R. (2009). Governance and Conservation of the Rapaz Khipu Patrimony. In D.F. Ruggles and H. Silverman (Eds.) *Intangible Heritage Embodied* (pp. 101-125). New York: Springer.

Van Hout, I. (2015). Museum Kapuas Raya: The in-between museum. In Paul Basu and Wayne Modest (Eds.) *Museums, heritage and international development* (pp. 180-197). Routledge.

Jerome McDonough: Tangible/Intangible: The Role of Libraries in the Preservation of Heritage

Richard Grounds, the director of the Yuchi Language Project, went to Philadelphia along with several other Yuchi to try to examine documentation on the Yuchi language held at the American Philosophical Society as part of their work on Yuchi language revitalization (Graham, 2009). The trip ended up being a good deal less than a success. The archive at the American Philosophical Society was only open to the public for a short period each day, and photocopying of the linguistic documentation in the archives was forbidden. They resorted to trying to photograph as many of the pages as they could in the limited time they had available, managing to photograph less than half of the documentation. When they returned home and read the information they had gathered to the elders still fluent in the language, they were discouraged to find only a small amount of the linguistic information they had gathered was actually new.

For those working with documentary materials in order to preserve intangible heritage, Grounds' experience may be far too familiar. Archives' and libraries' organization can seem arcane, and in many cases may seem to actively work against the use of materials by those seeking assistance in preserving intangible heritage. Donor agreements and intellectual property restrictions can significantly impede access to items in libraries and archives by communities who might put them to use. This is unfortunate, as the tangible materials held in libraries and archives could be of great help in preserving intangible forms of heritage. While Grounds found little of value at the American Philosophical Society, the Miami tribes of

Oklahoma and Indiana have based their language revitalization efforts on French/Miami-Illinois translation dictionaries from the 16th and 17th century Jesuits who documented the language; the dictionaries are currently housed in the libraries at Brown University and Trinity College in Hartford, and the Archives De La Compagnie de Jésus at St.-Jérôme, Québec. There are innumerable other examples where libraries and archives hold documentation that might assist in preservation of languages, crafts, performing arts, religious ceremonies, and other forms of intangible heritage.

Documentation of intangible heritage is not the intangible heritage itself, and preserving documentation is not the same thing as preserving intangible heritage. Preservation of intangible heritage requires enactment and the maintenance of that heritage as a lived experience. However, intangible heritage often draws upon tangible materials, and documentation of intangible heritage can contribute to maintenance of that heritage. Museums, libraries and archives all have a role to play in assisting communities of practice in preserving forms of intangible heritage. Unfortunately, libraries' and archives' ability to contribute to the preservation of intangible heritage is currently hampered by a number of factors.

Libraries and archives (unlike museums) are not particularly familiar with the concept of intangible heritage and generally do not see preserving it as part of their mission. Additionally, libraries and archives typically serve a narrowly defined, specific community, and the people who need their materials to assist in preserving intangible heritage may not be part of that community. While libraries and archives generally try to be at least somewhat helpful, the case of the American Philosophical Society above points to the problems that communities with intangible heritage may face in dealing with remote libraries and archives.

Another significant problem is that tangible materials which might assist in preserving intangible heritage can reside in a variety of different types of institutions, and libraries, archives and museums have had only limited success in cooperating on issues of collection development, access services, and means of discovery. Someone trying to identify and gain access to information regarding Washoku cooking, for example, might learn about physical items used in food preparation and serving at a museum, about recipes at a library, about the significance of certain foods or details on gathering and preparing ingredients from oral histories in an archive; but they will almost certainly not find anything which associates these diverse materials at different institutions with each other. Libraries, archives and museums divide up the world of tangible heritage in a way which is somewhat arbitrary, and that can impede those seeking to gather information regarding particular forms of intangible heritage.

Enlisting libraries and archives in efforts to preserve intangible heritage could be a boon to those endeavors, but research and a variety of practical steps will need to be undertaken before that coherence can be realized. On the practical side, libraries and archives need to reconsider access policies which unnecessarily restrict access to materials that can assist in preserving intangible heritage, particularly access for communities beyond their traditional areas of service. This might include considering potential contributions to the preservation of intangible heritage as a factor when evaluating which items they might wish to digitize and make available online. It should also include support for efforts to develop virtual collections of materials housed at multiple institutions that might contribute to preservation of particular forms of intangible heritage. Someone interested in kimchi-making as intangible heritage would certainly be interested in and likely to discover the resources of the Museum Kimchikan in Seoul, but less likely to find the 68 volumes on kimchi and its history at the Library of Congress, or the Southern Foodways Alliance's oral history taken from Yeon Ok Lee, a kimchi maker who works with the Kong Ju Korean Rice Cake company in Houston. Enabling cross-institutional discovery of such resources might be of great help to those working on the preservation of intangible culture.

There are also fundamental questions that need to be addressed to improve libraries' and archives' ability to contribute to the preservation of intangible heritage; and scholars in the fields of critical heritage studies, museum studies and library and information science should consider collaborating on such questions as:

- If libraries and archives are going to make decisions on collection development with the intent of supporting the preservation of intangible cultural heritage, how should those decisions be made? How can libraries and archives effectively work with communities possessing intangible heritage to make those decisions?

- Libraries, archives and museums have very different mechanisms for classification and access. How can we successfully integrate those to improve access to intangible heritage documentation and other materials which might support ICH preservation?

- What social/political/financial obstacles impede the collaboration of libraries, archives and museums on these issues? How might they be addressed?

Libraries and archives have enough experience in the preservation of tangible materials to know that preservation is never easy, nor cheap; and it is to the benefit of their institutions, and the communities they serve, if they collaborate on developing solutions to the problems of preservation. Libraries and archives can contribute to the preservation of intangible heritage, but if that contribution is to be realized, they must engage with both the museum community and scholars in the field of critical heritage studies to make it happen.

References

Graham, Laura (2009). "Problematizing technologies for documenting intangible culture: Some positive and negative consequences." In D. Fairchild Ruggles and Helaine Silverman (Eds.) *Intangible heritage embodied* (pp. 185-200). New York: Springer.

Gabriel B. Tait: Heritage Studies and Photojournalism: Questions and Reflections for the 21st Century Scholar

Through photojournalism, scholars and practitioners have a unique tool to integrate the visual with their traditional textual fieldnotes and participant observational techniques. Through photojournalism, Michele Dominy (1993) posits, one's heritage and culture is revealed in a contextual and comprehensive manor. Finally, it is presented that photojournalism provides scholars and practitioners the academic space to document, reflect, and ask questions about their own heritage and culture in what they see. To accomplish these points, we explore a few practical questions that one must ask when incorporating the camera into their research. I offer a case study from my time working as a photojournalist at the *St. Louis Post-Dispatch*. Finally, I offer a few reflective and ethical considerations when applying photojournalism techniques to research.

Questions

It is vital to ask questions about how photojournalism might reveal one's heritage. Additionally, it's important to consider the role which *seeing* one's heritage plays in helping outsiders process (a) what they are seeing; (b) what cultural cues are present in the photographs being presented;

(c) what ethical challenges arise when using a camera; and (d) how scholars may engage local communities to have them photograph their own
heritage.

Case Study: Walking in the Best Shoes

When I worked as a photojournalist for the *St. Louis Post-Dispatch* from
2002-2007, it was common for our assignment editor to distribute the
day's shooting schedule. The schedule let each photojournalist know the
assignments they would be working on. One of my stories was to document a community supermarket that had served its Central West End customers since 1901. Since there was a looming grocery strike, the newspaper wanted to develop a repository of photographs before the strike
happened.

My first photographs were exteriors of the building and general cus-
tomer traffic. I aimed to show where the market was located in relation to
other landmarks. I also wanted to show the customers — what they were
wearing and how they contributed to the life of this century-old establishment. I entered the market and started walking the aisles before taking
additional pictures.

As I walked, I repeatedly asked myself: What makes this market a staple
in the community? What became strikingly apparent as I moved back and
forth were the customers. The people were eclectic. Some wore their hats
to the back. Others had colorful jackets and scarves. But the person I
thought best represented the supermarket's tone was a man who graced
the aisles with his long slender legs. They were tanned. He was wearing a
white knit beret, white shorts, and a white sleeved shirt. As he studied the
bottles of wine, holding his cup of coffee, other shoppers also took notice
of him. This elderly man was wearing a pair of women's heeled slip-on
shoes. The shoes were dark colored, and his feet were large.

Upon further investigation I learned the man was 69 years old, a former audio engineer, and long-time resident of the community. His family
members were the founders of a quarry which they still operate on the
Mississippi river. He also shared that he owned over 20 pairs of women's
shoes, and that his most expensive was a $600 pair of Italian boots.

The interaction reminded me how much of our history is preserved by
what we see and how we process what has been observed. Heritage can be
synonymous with community. When a photojournalist goes out into the
community and makes photographs, it is their responsibility to understand
the context they are photographing.

Newspaper readers as well as his fellow shoppers do double takes when they see Albert "Al" Bussen Jr. This photo of Bussen, 69, was published in September. A retired audio engineer, Bussen simply loves to wear women's shoes — and he does, wherever he goes. Gabriel B. Tait | Post-Dispatch

This photograph was published twice (September and December 2005) in the *St. Louis Post-Dispatch* in St. Louis, Missouri. Photo by: Gabriel B. Tait.

Takeaways

The 69-year-old man at the supermarket represents a microcosm of the Central West End community: an affluent, socially progressive, and trendy area of St. Louis.

When considering what role seeing one's heritage plays in helping outsiders process what they are seeing, the photograph of the man reveals an aspect of his identity; thus part of his culture is seen. The cultural cues presented in the photograph vary. We see the African American man with his hat to the back. This generally represents an urban context. The lady in the background may indicate an inclusivity in the general location. The people are in an aisle that has wine and spirits on the store shelves. This cue can indicate this community's understanding of alcoholic beverages in the market. If one is from a state or county that does not allow the selling of alcohol, the photograph serves as an important resource for understanding. The main subject is wearing white. White has symbolic meaning of purity in some cultures. The man is also wearing shoes that are generally considered out of the cultural norm for his gender. His love for women's shoes, and the glaring of shoppers in the market, shows that there may be some questions. But the photographer's pictures are respectful of the various cultural norms. Collier (2009) rightly observes how these cues obtained from the camera reveal, "complex spatial and material elements" (13) that should assist researchers and viewers.

Ethical Considerations

There are a number of ethical challenges that arise when using a camera. In this case, the photojournalist must remain as photographically neutral as possible. Photojournalism is about documenting real life situations without directly influencing them. The photojournalist may never stage an image or ask the subject to do something that would alter the real meaning of the context. The photojournalist must never exoticize their subjects. Ultimately the guiding ethical principles for photojournalists using their art to document heritage and culture can be found in the National Press Photographers Association Code Of Ethics (2017).

Conclusion

When a researcher and/or photojournalist goes out into a community they are committing to systematically capture some of the most meaningful aspects of their subjects' lives. The publications of these images become spectral ships for others who wish to look back at the historic contexts and interrogate what is seen. If photojournalism is going to become meaningful in Heritage and Cultural Studies, scholars must commit themselves to understanding how the camera becomes a significant tool in their research toolbox. Shoot on!

References

Collier, M. (2013). "Photographic Exploration of Social and Cultural Experience." In *Viewpoints: Visual Anthropologists at Work* Mary Strong and Laena Wilder (Eds.) Austin TX: University of Texas Press (13-32).

Dominy, M. D. (1993). "Photojournalism, Anthropology, and Ethnographic Authority." *Cultural Anthropology*: 8(3), 317–337.

Bryan Moore: Heritage Studies and Rhetorical Theory: The Rhetoric of Place

My main link with Heritage Studies is by way of a course in our program I taught called The Rhetoric of Place. As most readers know, the word "rhetoric" can mean almost anything, and the word "place" is even more vague, since *anywhere* is a place. In my initial planning, it seemed sometimes that the course might more properly be called *The Anything of Anywhere*. But a large part of the pleasure of the planning was in discovering what a course with such a title means. I tend toward a classical view of rhetoric as the art of persuasion, both as a means of creating ideas and "arguments" and, perhaps more importantly, as a critical tool for analyzing how texts in a wide sense of the word operate. Rhetorical theory is rooted largely in Aristotle, though the field has, over the centuries, expanded greatly and become an appropriation, interrogation, and dismantling of his theories. Since rhetorical contexts are, as Kenneth Burke writes, continually born anew, other rhetorics, including relatively recent ones — those of Burke, Ernest Bormann, Michel Foucault, and bell hooks, all of whose theories we discussed — provide rich frameworks in helping to understand how texts operate.

In the course we looked at a fairly wide array of texts on place — narratives, essays, and a little fiction (I am otherwise a literature teacher) — in a variety of locations, mostly in the United States. One of the challenges to the course is delineating, where possible, the differences between place and *space*, a term that would potentially make an already wide course content so wide that it would disappear. I was not able to fully make this neat delineation when we discussed, for example, bell hooks on the need for black people, and black women in particular, to find a "space of resistance" outside of white control. I wanted, though, to keep the course centered mostly on geographical places. So I ventured rather widely, from the New York Bowery in the late nineteenth century (Jacob Riis and Stephen Crane), to the streets of Paris with Georg Simmel, to the more recent New York of Michel de Certeau, to Mike Davis's militarized Los Angeles landscape, the Devil's Highway of Luis Alberto Urrea, and on to regional, rural areas presented by several writers, including Mary E. Wilkins Freeman, Sarah Orne Jewett, and Shirley Abbott.

My own scholarly interests are centered especially on the rhetoric of wilderness areas, places that, by definition, are characterized by a small to nonexistent human footprint. It is not a given that everyone acknowledges or understands the need for wilderness, but it *is* something that may be and has been defended on a number of fronts. Wild places are treasured, of course, for their scenery, for recreation, for their spiritual, aesthetic, and cultural values. Among the latter we can include heritage: as a species we have lived in the wilds, or relative wilds, a thousand times longer than in civilization. (And maybe longer than that: recently, paleontologists found in Morocco human skulls from 300,000 or more years ago — 100,000 years earlier than previously thought.) Wilderness is a major factor in the shaping of culture, and it remains the only (large) physical option for escaping the control of institutional and commercial powers. The wilds help us understand the source of freedom, as Frederick Jackson Turner wrote in 1893. Thoreau wrote in *Walden* that "Our village life would stagnate if it were not for the unexplored forests and meadows that surround it. We need the tonic of wildness . . ." (317); and in a late essay, "Walking," he wrote the much-discussed phrase, "in Wildness is the preservation of the world" (202). Such ideas are at least as relevant today as in the nineteenth century, though I fear we as a nation are losing this idea amidst a barrage of technophilic, commercial, and political interests. I believe that the most vital argument for wilderness lies in its intrinsic worth, one that is largely outside of human operations, or not especially *for* humans at least. Animals, flora, rocks, and bodies of water deserve to operate because nature, or God, put them there, and most of these were there long before we were.

The preservation of wilderness areas is itself an enormous challenge for those working in heritage professions, and this is outside of my purview as a scholar. "What *is* wilderness?" is a question that is controversial on a number of points, and the (mostly) white determination of what is "natural" continues to come into conflict with the heritage of a number of indigenous peoples. Some have argued that the idealization of the wilderness as unpeopled landscapes has, on occasion, "overlooked the socioeconomic implications of such an ideal and the interests of the peoples who relied on those lands for their welfare, including Native American, rural American, and indigenous peoples abroad" (J.M. Turner 258). For American Indians, the concept of wilderness is a European idea that, at least up to the near present, has been used to erase their memory from the land. As one Indian rights activist stated, "There was no wilderness until the Whites arrived" (Miller 109).

Yet wilderness was a small part of our course content. I was less interested in promoting my interests than in helping the students explore their own academic and vocational interests. The students applied course material to a wonderfully impressive array of subjects, including the rhetoric of place in the preservation of local historical sites, regional Confederate Monuments, and the pre-civil rights *Negro Motorist Green Book*. I tried hard to do my part, but any success in the course was the result of some bright, hardworking students.

Near the end of the course we read works by Martha Nussbaum and Kwame Anthony Appiah on cosmopolitanism, which is one possible rhetorical stance regarding globalization, a phenomenon that, Appiah writes, is nothing all that new. He quotes the ancient Roman writer Terence: "I am human; nothing human is alien to me." The Greek Cynic philosopher Diogenes, who claimed himself "a citizen of the world," is often seen as the first cosmopolitan, and the idea received much of its philosophical basis in the writings of Kant, though he himself didn't venture far from Königsberg. Nussbaum warns against the unexamined feeling that one's own preferences and ways are neutral and natural, when in fact we are all subject to the accident of birth. By looking at ourselves through cosmopolitan eyes, we come to see that our practices are local and unessential to humanity.

References

Appiah, Kwame Anthony. *Cosmopolitanism: Ethics in a World of Strangers.* New York: Norton, 2006.
Burke, Kenneth. *A Rhetoric of Motives.* Berkeley: U of California P, 1969.
"Diogenes." In *The Cynic Philosophers from Diogenes to Julian.* Trans. Robert Dobbin. London: Penguin, 2012. 28-60.
hooks, bell. "Closing the Margin as a Space of Radical Openness." In *Yearning: Race, Gender, and Cultural Politics.* Boston: South End, 1990. 145-54.
Miller, Angela. "The Fate of Wilderness in American Landscape Art: The

Dilemmas of Nature's Nation." In *American Wilderness: A New History*. Ed. Michael Lewis. Oxford: Oxford UP, 2007. 91-112.

Nussbaum, Martha C. "Reply." In *For Love of Country?* Ed. Joshua Cohen. Boston: Beacon, 1996. 131-44.

Thoreau, Henry David. *Walden*. Princeton: Princeton UP, 1971.

—. "Walking." In *Excursions*. Ed. Joseph J. Moldenhauer. Princeton: Princeton UP, 2007. 185-222.

Turner, Frederick Jackson. *The Frontier in American History*. New York: Henry Holt, 1920.

Turner, James Morton. "The Politics of Modern Wilderness." In *American Wilderness: A New History*. Ed. Michael Lewis. Oxford: Oxford UP, 2007. 243-61.

Kirstin C. Erickson: Heritage and Foodways Studies: Cuisine, Memory, and Belonging in Hispano New Mexico

On each of the nine nights leading up to Christmas, in the churches at the center of social and religious life in the Hispanic mountain villages of northern New Mexico, community members gather to celebrate the tradition of *Las Posadas*, which recalls the plight of Mary and Joseph in search of shelter on the eve of Christ's birth. Congregants join two teen-agers, costumed as the Holy Couple, in a call-and-response re-enactment of their quest for lodging. While the sacred drama and Mass are enjoyed as a special ending to the advent season, for many, the definitive climax of each evening is the feast that follows the service. At this potluck meal, guests are treated to delicate *biscochitos* (anise-flavored shortbread cookies), *pozole* (hominy stew) with dollops of *chile colorado* (red chile sauce), green chile chicken enchiladas, *chicos* (tender kernels of corn roasted, dried, and reconstituted in broth), *menudo* (tripe soup), *sopa* (bread pudding), and *natillas* (cinnamon custard). These are some of the "traditional dishes" most associated with Hispano identity and heritage – carefully prepared by local families and awaited with great anticipation. The consumption of this elaborate meal is accompanied by conversation about recipes passed down, the sourcing of regionally-unique ingredients, and stories about parents, grandparents, and the past.

My work on Hispano foodways is part of a larger project on material

109

culture, memory, and the politics of representation in northern New Mexico. I find the insights of critical heritage studies particularly useful to my own understanding of these questions. While anthropologist and museum studies specialist Sharon Macdonald stresses the inseparability of heritage from memory and identity, calling our attention to the "memory-heritage-identity complex" (2013:5), she also highlights memory's divergence from heritage, stating, "Where 'memory' entices social researchers into analogies with individual memory and the language of psychology and also prompts questions about veracity and transmission, 'heritage' directs attention to materiality, durability over time and value" (2013:17). Critical heritage studies – the "interrogation of why and how some things come to count as 'heritage,' and the consequences that flow from this" (Macdonald 2013:17) – is interdisciplinary at its core. In this essay, I will discuss just a few of the ways in which folklorists, anthropologists, historians, sociologists, and specialists in tourism theory and museum studies contribute to a critical heritage perspective on foodways and inform my own endeavors to understand Nuevomexicano culinary practices as vital modes of "past presencing" (Macdonald 2013:80).

In Hispanic New Mexico, where most people hail from a Catholic background and self-identify as *Hispano* Spanish American, or *Nuevomexicano*, foodways inscribe the boundaries of identity. "Meatless" dishes served on Good Friday, for instance, include salmon loaf and *paella*, but also feature the distinctive norteño specialties, *tortas de huevo* (fluffy egg fritters floating in red chile sauce) and *panocha* (sprouted wheat pudding). Here, foods that are identified as "traditional" are imbued with an intense locality, materializing cultural memory and belonging. Hispanos seek to emphasize their 300-year presence in New Mexico and to differentiate themselves as unique among Latinos. Restaurants popular among local patrons feature lamb *costillas* (ribs), smoky chicos, and *sopaipillas* (fried bread drizzled with honey) in addition to tamales and burritos. Anthropologists Michael Di Giovine and Ronda Brulotte examine how people deploy "elements of their foodways to distinguish themselves from their neighbors – problematizing, in the process the constructed notion of a 'national' or otherwise 'ethnic' food" (2014:6); and historian Jeffrey Pilcher's work unpacks the complexities of regional differentiation in Southwestern cuisine (2001).

Insights generated by critical tourism studies are particularly salient in New Mexico, where chile festivals draw tourist dollars and the key decision restaurant patrons encounter when ordering a meal is "Red or green [chile]?" Likewise, the *biscochito*, a signature treat offered at restaurants, sold in gift shops, and served at weddings, has since 1989 been recognized as the "state cookie" of New Mexico. Cultural tourism is one of the pillars

of New Mexico's modern economy, and culinary heritage is part of that cal-
culus. While the ability to satisfy tourists' desire for "authentic" cuisine
may result in tangible economic benefits (Pilcher 2004:93), it is also the
case that formerly obscure foodways or partially "invented" culinary traditions, spurred by the demands of tourism, may be expanded and promoted
as heritage, becoming regional icons of a greater national patrimony (Brulotte and Starkman 2014:116-118). Gastronomic tourism may precipitate
cultural revitalization or the valorization of foods once considered unre-
markable (Di Giovine 2014); indeed, as folklorist Lucy Long points out,
"while an activity may be rendered meaningless through the commodifi-
cation and adaptation that occurs with tourism, that same tourism 'can
engender processes of reflection that lead to cultural elaboration'" (Greenwood 1989:185 cited in Long 2004:6).

Anthropologist C. Nadia Seremetakis observes, "nothing tastes as good
as the past" (1994:1). In New Mexico, flavors and aromas are integral to
place-bound memories. When I asked an interlocutor if I could interview
her about childhood memories and local history, her response was telling:
she invited me to her house and taught me how to seed and roast chiles
and then reconstitute them with water, garlic, and oregano, to make the
sauce known as *chile caribe*, a local favorite. She remembered the chiles
her father grew on their farm: "We roasted them in the *horno*. And they
smelled so good!" She spoke longingly of the color, scent, and weight of
the *ristras*, strings of chiles hung to dry around her girlhood home in preparation for market. Anthropologist Jon Holtzman examines how taste and
aroma can trigger deep memories. He contends that memories associated
with food are anchored in the "sensorial experience of eating" and reveal
an important "contrast between discursive and practical memory" (Holtzman 2009:33). David Sutton posits that "food's memory power derives in
part from synesthesia . . . the synthesis or crossing of experiences from
different sensory registers (i.e. taste, smell, hearing)" (2001:17).

Folklorist and performance studies scholar Barbara Kirshenblatt-Gimblett maintains, "Not only do food experiences organize and integrate a
particularly complex set of sensory and social experiences in distinctive
ways, but also they form edible chronotopes (sensory space-time convergences)" (2004: xiii). I contend it is crucial to understand a cuisine's affective value – and its capacity for emplacement – in tandem. Here enters
the concept of *terroir*, which anthropologist Amy Trubek calls the "taste
of place" (2008). Trubek explains, "The regional foods ... make up a
cuisine du terroir taste of the land from which they come" (2008:152). Di
Giovine and Brulotte explain that while "*terroir* designations have emerged
precisely because of economic concerns," a "protected mark" is useful for

staking an exclusive claim to place-based produce (2014:8). "One can cogently construct, and argue for, the application of *terroir* designations for many culinary traditions – even when many of the practitioners themselves do not readily use such idioms" (2014:10). Sociologist Erika Derkas observes that Nuevomexicano foodways "developed in response to a physical environment that is relatively unsympathetic," characterized by "high elevations, extreme water limitations, and arid soils" (2014). Foodways developed under these same tough conditions in Colorado's San Luis Valley (which shares northern New Mexico's cultural history) feature prominently in the evocative food-centered life histories collected by anthropologist Carole Counihan (2009). Derkas explains that seed saving, preservation, canning, steaming, and specialized drying techniques are all cultural responses to the demands of the land (2014). And nothing epitomizes Nuevomexicano *terroir* more than the smoky flavor of chicos and "the real Chimayó chile," a small pepper that grows in the high-altitude, stream-fed Chimayó valley. The land-inflected flavors of chicos and Chimayó chiles become heightened signifiers of survival and of the bond between heritage and place.

   Chiles, chicos, panocha and *natillas* entangle consumption, memory and *terroir* – or even more fundamentally, the physical, affective and cognitive. Critical heritage studies provides a means to understand these relationships, offering perspectives as to why Hispanos spend so much time talking about food, flavor, land, the provenance of ingredients, and methods of preparing dishes "the old way." As Barbara Kirshenblatt-Gimblett contends, "heritage produces something new in the present that has recourse to the past" (1998:149). Amidst northern New Mexico's contemporary economic struggles, increasing outmigration, and dependence on cultural tourism, Hispano self-definitions of identity, the cultivation of memory, and claims to place appear more pressing than ever. What elements, tangible and intangible, are selected in this process of self-representation? And who has the power to make those choices? Heritage studies, the examination of how people marshal the past to constitute meaningful worlds in the present, provides an insightful intervention.

References

Brulotte, Ronda L. and Alvin Starkman (2014). Caldo de Piedra and claiming pre-Hispanic cuisine as cultural heritage. In Ronda L. Brulotte and Michael A. Di Giovine (Eds.) *Edible identities: Food as cultural heritage* (pp. 109-123). New York: Routledge.

Brulotte, Ronda L. and Michael A. Di Giovine (Eds.). (2014). *Edible identities: Food as cultural heritage*. New York: Routledge.

Counihan, Carole M. (2009). *A tortilla is like life: Food and culture in the San Luis Valley of Colorado.* Austin: University of Texas Press.

Derkas, Erika (2014 Spring). New Mexican chiles: Sentinels of Hispano identity and cultural heritage. *Digest: A Journal of Foodways and Culture* 2(2). Online publication URL: http://digest.champlain.edu/vol2_issue2/article2_2_2.html#18.

Di Giovine, Michael A. (2014). The everyday as extraordinary: Revitalization, religion, and the elevation of Cucina Casareccia to heritage cuisine in Pietrelcina, Italy. In Ronda L. Brulotte and Michael A. Di Giovine (Eds.) *Edible Identities: Food as Cultural Heritage* (pp. 77-92). New York: Routledge.

Di Giovine, Michael A. and Ronda L. Brulotte (2014). Introduction: Food and Foodways as Cultural Heritage. In Ronda L. Brulotte and Michael A. Di Giovine (Eds.) *Edible identities: Food as cultural heritage* (pp. 1-27). New York: Routledge.

Greenwood, Davydd (1989). Culture by the pound: An anthropological perspective on tourism as culture commoditization. In Valene L. Smith (Ed.) *Hosts and guests: The anthropology of tourism* (2nd ed.). (pp. 171-185). Philadelphia: University of Pennsylvania Press.

Holtzman, Jon (2009). *Uncertain tastes: Memory, ambivalence, and the politics of eating in Samburu, Northern Kenya.* Berkeley: University of California Press.

Kirshenblatt-Gimblett, Barbara (1998). *Destination culture: Tourism, museums, and heritage.* Berkeley: University of California Press.

——————— (2004). Foreword. In Lucy M. Long (Ed.) *Culinary tourism* (pp. xi-xiv). Lexington: University Press of Kentucky.

Long, Lucy M., (Ed.). (2004). *Culinary tourism.* Lexington: University Press of Kentucky.

——————— (2004). Introduction. In Lucy M. Long (Ed.) *Culinary Tourism* (pp. 1-19). Lexington: University Press of Kentucky.

Macdonald, Sharon (2013). *Memorylands: Heritage and identity in Europe today.* New York: Routledge.

Pilcher, Jeffrey M. (2001). Tex-Mex, Cal-Mex, New Mex, or Whose Mex? Notes on the historical geography of Southwestern cuisine. *Journal of the Southwest* 43(4): 659-679.

——————— (2004). From "Montezuma's Revenge" to "Mexican Truffles": Culinary tourism across the Rio Grande. In Lucy M. Long (Ed.) *Culinary tourism* (pp. 76-96). Lexington: University Press of Kentucky.

Seremetakis, C. Nadia. (1994a). The Memory of the senses, part I: Marks of the transitory. In C. Nadia Seremetakis (Ed.) *The Senses still:*

Perception and memory as material culture in modernity (pp. 1-18). Chicago: University of Chicago Press.

Sutton, David E. (2001). *Remembrance of repasts: An anthropology of food and memory.* New York: Berg.

Trubek, Amy B. (2008). *The Taste of place: A cultural journey into Terroir.* Berkeley: University of California Press.

Thomas Walker: Critical Heritage Studies and Environmental Studies

A convergence of critical heritage studies with environmental humanities makes the interconnectedness and meanings of place and space thinkable and productive in exciting new ways. 'Conservation' and 'preservation' are already part of a shared lexicon of sustainability in cultural, historical, and environmental discourses, and are distinguished by an otherwise historical frame of mind creating discontinuities and exclusions. As Jeff Todd Titan, notes:

> Ever since the early Enlightenment, preservation and conservation have been closely related. Taken as near synonyms, their meaning is to maintain an object or system insofar as possible in its present state, to protect it from change, usually for contemplation, research, display, and perhaps for use. (Titon 2015: 160)

While conservationists, Titon continues, emphasize restoration, and preservationists the goal of preserving original conditions, these distinctions are context- or discipline-specific, and involve different degrees of interference or intervention. More radical interventions among the so-called new conservationists of recent vintage emphasize the ingenuity, development, and expansion of cultural carrying capacity to engineer and manage "a planet transformed by the artificial ecosystems required to sustain" growing populations (Ellis 2015: 26). But whatever the terms and distinctions, the scale, context, and human dimensions of conservation and preservation offer multiple frameworks and perspectives on meaning. What relevance, we ask, does critical heritage studies have to environmental studies? Where in this broad interdisciplinary confluence, ranging from humanities to sciences, are the current intersections and articulations?

'Human dimensions' is a term used in environmental studies with a social science and humanities emphasis. Just as with landscapes, parks, and preserves, for instance, we talk not only about the rationale, strategies, and mechanisms for their conservation, or the ways in which power and culture are embedded in landscape, but also about social impacts and the way in which protected areas or other features of our environments produce place, space, and people, including inequalities and dispossessions. Protected areas matter, as Paige West, et. al. (2006) argues, because they are a way of seeing, understanding, and (re)producing the world.

The same, I think, can be said of watersheds. While a watershed is physically the area of land that sheds or drains water in the hydrologic area or region to a single destination — into a river or basin, or onward to the sea — it is also the basis for a different kind of social organization, one that supersedes, in fact *precedes*, municipal, county, and state infrastructure. The concept of 'thinking like a watershed,' coined by aural historian Jack Loeffler (2012), suggests new responsibilities concerning social relationships and land stewardship.

Some of these new responsibilities and perspectives are represented in community-based conservation which seeks to balance, for instance, preservation and sustainable use. Research in community-based conservation is social-ecological in approach: people are seen to be integral to the dynamics of ecosystems rather than merely managers or stressors. This development recognizes the value of traditional knowledge in a globalizing world, drawing upon all sources of ecological knowledge and decentering expert-based approaches within broader stakeholder knowledge networks. In these frameworks, local culture, heritage, and Traditional Ecological Knowledge (TEK) are complementary, and mutually reinforce some variant of conservation or preservation ethics.

Focusing on a few convergences within this framework, one cannot fail to recognize weather-related impacts in the organizing and thinking taking place around the vulnerabilities of landscapes, and particularly built environments. Annapolis, for example, is one among many coastal communities now with hazard mitigation plans to address community response to sea level rise and its impact on its historic waterfront. In Miami, community activists are organizing against climate gentrification, as the high ground there — a mere fifteen feet above sea level — is home to Miami's historic black communities in neighborhoods like Liberty City.

While these two examples illustrate organized responses to impending natural disasters and imminent displacement and dispossession, they hint at conflicts over land use, property rights, and cultural values.

A striking, perhaps now well-known case that brought into play open conflicts between environmentalist and native notions of cultural heritage and sustainability was the Makah tradition of gray whale hunting. This controversial story, of a Pacific Northwest tribe with a centuries-old whaling tradition suddenly thrust onto the world stage in 1999, pitched local tradition against environmental conservation. For the Makah, the whale was a symbol of cultural identity, and its place in their diet represented indigenous cultural survival. Tribal leaders asserted a right to conserve their heritage. For animal rights and other anti-whaling environmentalists, however, the grey whale was proxy for species extinction as they asserted their moral claims over the Makah cultural claims. The grey whale served in a sense as the pivot for competing and opposing critiques of modernity and survival (Baron and Walker forthcoming).

Viewed through another lens, however, one could argue that the Makah revival of whaling in 1999 testified to their cultural resilience; it included significant adaptation of their traditional culture to technological change. While this view is all but lost in the highly publicized conflict, it ties to examples of more collaborative successes in community-based conservation. One of these is a collaborative research model I worked on involving the San Diego Sea Urchin divers who created a Barefoot Ecology Program, working with scientists from UC Santa Barbara.

This program enabled working divers to gather scientifically sound data on the sea urchin population; *and* their association represented the industry's interest in collaborative management, research, and monitoring because it provided the most effective and resilient strategy to anticipate fluctuations in the sea urchin market. It helped compensate for the data-poor, state-based regulatory and management regimes. This exemplifies the practice of resilience in an unstable fishery. It demonstrates economic coordination with local knowledge, and it recognizes a discourse of regulatory authority and governance with non-traditional actors across multiple scales — ranging from local conditions in the kelp forests around San Diego Harbor to market conditions in upscale sushi bars in Tokyo. The fishery is still regulated as a marine protected area (MPA), as designated by the California Department of Fish and Wildlife. From a fisheries management point of view, these kinds of collaborative arrangements are directed at maintaining sustainability in fish stocks. But it is clear, too, that local knowledge, even if narrowly documented, plays an increasingly key role in the decentering of expertise.

It thus maintains a livelihood and creates a value for local ecological knowledge. The west coast sea urchin fishery only dates to the 1970s, but examples of what is more commonly called 'traditional ecological knowledge' are increasingly recognized in natural resources conservation as well as in cultural heritage conservation — for example, in the traditional fisheries of Palau (Johannes 1981), the artisanal cheesemaking shops in the Italian Alps (Grasseni 2012), landraces in the Pyrenees (Reyes-García 2014), and the famous Balinese water temples where irrigation management in rice paddy ecosystems has earned a World Heritage status.

I conclude with a story from my fieldwork from several years ago when I was working in the Delmarva peninsula. Because Delmarva is a wetland region, I was working mostly with hunters, trappers, and watermen; I became interested in differences in ways of knowing — between the traditional marshland culture and the regulatory state. I met a hunter/trapper who summed up the century-old relationship of hunters and game wardens or conservationists as a conflict in ways of knowing. Wardens and environmentalists, to him, were simply "educated beyond their intelligence."

To him, there was a dual and competing vision for conservation, and he noted how exogenous rules had prevailed and how local culture was disparaged with the imposition of one system of knowledge over another — a kind of epistemic injustice. But in this culture, in tales of hunters outwitting game wardens, there were stories and memories about conflicts with the law and with environmental regulations. To be sure, there were always hunters among the wardens, but the more interesting stories were those tracking the movement of history and belief, and care and duty of place, in the everyday lives of local residents throughout Delmarva's wetlands.

One story he told was about a notorious market gunner named Mark Daisy. According to the story, Mark Daisy is bragging in a bar one evening about all the ducks he bagged in a single day, well beyond the limit. He is of course overheard by a couple of undercover wardens who proceed to try to arrest him. But in the end he is vindicated by his reputation as the biggest liar on Chincoteague. "Everyone here," he says, "will tell you I'm the biggest liar on Chincoteague."

In this story, local poetics and tradition trump the regulatory state. But the larger story of intangible cultural heritage is the one in which local culture, prior to market gunning, cultivated over generations a land ethic in sustainable relationship with natural resources. At the turn of the last century the Eastern shore increasingly became a tourist destination for hunting parties from major urban areas in the mid-Atlantic region— Philadelphia, Baltimore, Washington, New York, etc. The law that created the outlaw gunner was the Federal Migratory Bird Act of 1918. But it was the attraction to the region of wealthy sports hunters who created the market gunner and the local businesses to support it. Excessive slaughter of waterfowl, in turn, drove market gunning to the limits of the ecological carrying capacity and led to the imposition of federal regulations to protect the resource. Local residents who for generations relied on fishing and hunting and trapping for subsistence no longer had the freedom to exercise local customary sustainability practice without regulatory oversight.

References

Baron, Robert and Thomas Walker (Forthcoming). Sustainability clashes and concordances. In Timothy J. Cooley (Ed.), *Cultural sustainabilities: Music, media, language, advocacy*. Urbana: University of Illinois Press.

Ellis, Erle C. (2015). Too big for nature. In Ben A. Minter and Stephen J. Pyne (Eds.), *After preservation: Saving American nature in the age of humans*. Chicago: University of Chicago Press.

Grasseni, Christina (2012). Developing cheese at the foot of the Alps. In Elizabeth Finnis (Ed.), *Reimagining marginalized foods*. Tucson: University of Arizona Press.

Johannes, R. E. (1981). *Words of the lagoon: Fishing and marine lore in the Palau district of Micronesia*. Berkeley: University of California Press.

Loeffler, Jack and Celestia Loeffler (Eds.). (2012). *Thinking like a watershed: Voices from the West*. Albuquerque: University of New Mexico Press.

Reyes-García, Victoria (2014). The Values of traditional knowledge systems. Public presentation, National Socio-Environmental Synthesis Center. Annapolis. MD.

Titon, Jeff Todd (2015). Sustainability, resilience, and adaptive management for applied ethnomusicology. In Svanibor Pettan and Jeff Todd Titon (Eds.). *The Oxford handbook of applied ethnomusicology*. Oxford and New York: Oxford University Press.

West, Paige, James Igoe, and Dan Brockington (2006). Parks and peoples: The social impact of protected areas. *Annual Review of Anthropology* 35:251–77.

Barry Bergey: Intangible Cultural Heritage: Policies, Programs, Prospects

The following address was delivered at the "États généraux du patrimoine immatérial au Québec" meeting of the Conseil Québécois du Patrimoine Vivant, Québec City, Canada, March 20-23, 2014.

Thank you so much for inviting me to this meeting and allowing me to add my voice to this conversation on intangible cultural heritage. I am Barry Bergey and I direct the Folk & Traditional Arts program at the National Endowment for the Arts in the United States. First, I need to say that the opinions I express are solely my own – my perspectives do not represent in an official capacity the views of the National Endowment for the Arts or the United States Government.

This leads to a second point of note. I couldn't speak for the U.S. government, even if I wanted to. The United States does not have a Ministry of Culture, so no one governmental body is solely responsible for making and executing cultural policy and thus no single voice speaks on behalf of our nation's cultural portfolio. At least four governmental entities have significant responsibilities for issues related to intangible cultural heritage (ICH). The National Endowment for the Arts, where I work, is primarily a funding body tasked with financially supporting arts programs through not-for-profit organizations (NGO's) and state and regional arts agencies. Funding for the agency comes from federally appropriated tax dollars. Our sister agency, the National Endowment for the Humanities, supports the study of the arts, history, and cultural heritage, among the other humanities, through grants to cultural institutions, individual scholars, and state humanities councils. The Institute for Museums and Library Services supports activities and programs of museums and libraries across the country.

The Library of Congress serves as our national library and it also houses the U.S. Copyright Office and is the repository for all copyrighted material. A fifth entity, the Smithsonian Institution, is not a government agency but rather a public trust that receives a significant portion of its funding from the Congress, and it is the world's largest complex of museums and research facilities; and its mission includes understanding, preserving, and presenting our nation's cultural heritage.

While each of these entities has intangible cultural heritage within its purview, none acts as a central policy-making body when it comes to cultural heritage. In fact some observers have pointed out that when it comes to culture, the U.S. policy is to not have a policy. One might say that our policy is as decentralized and diverse as our intangible cultural heritage. Each of the aforementioned institutions plays its own unique role with regard to culture, a role more easily described in programmatic terms rather than through policy instruments. As if this weren't confusing enough, I should also say that the term "intangible cultural heritage" is not commonly used in the United States. More frequently the terms folk and traditional arts, folk culture, folklore, or living cultural heritage are used to describe what the UNESCO convention defines as intangible cultural heritage and I will sometimes use these terms interchangeably as I speak.

As background, I will say just a little about roles of these various governmental bodies with regard to intangible cultural heritage. A Memorandum of Understanding, first signed in 1981 and renewed and revised in 2001, outlines the roles of four of the primary institutions addressing "American folk culture." It states that: the National Endowment for the Arts provides funding support for the presentation of folk artists, documentation of folk artists through fieldwork, education, archival preservation, recognition of master folk artists, and support for a national infrastructure of folk arts specialists; the National Endowment for the Humanities "awards grants to support and promote scholarly research, education and public programs in the humanities, as well as preservation of materials important to research, education, and public understanding of the humanities, as related to folk culture;" the American Folklife Center at the Library of Congress preserves and presents American folklife through programs, publications, and its archival collections; and the Center for Folklife and Cultural Heritage at the Smithsonian Institution produces the annual Smithsonian Folklife Festival held on our National Mall, conducts research and maintains archival materials, and produces recordings, exhibitions, and documentary media. While there is some overlap in certain areas, these individual entities each play an important and distinct role in safeguarding intangible cultural heritage.

Several common threads or strategies characterize the work of all of these institutions when it comes to safeguarding cultural heritage: 1) *discovery* – the need continually to do fieldwork (inventories) to identify artists and cultural communities, especially given our mobile and newcomer populations; 2) *collaboration* – the importance of working with cultural communities and the responsibility to respect the views of culture bearers and to understand the social, cultural, and historic context of their work; 3) *education* – the necessity of fostering understanding of cultural traditions and of encouraging the perpetuation of cultural knowledge and skills; and 4) *diversity* – the awareness that there are multiple aesthetic traditions and standards of excellence when working with culturally distinct communities.

Given those assumptions, I will spend most of the rest of my presentation speaking about practice – the programs and the strategies rather than policies — that we use to address intangible cultural heritage at the National Endowment for the Arts. There are five primary strategies that characterize the work of the NEA in safeguarding intangible cultural heritage: 1) support for the public presentation of folk arts, through festivals, tours, exhibitions, and media presentations; 2) support for fieldwork and documentation of folk artists and folk arts activities; 3) support for a network of folk arts specialists based in state, regional, and local arts agencies, as well as other partnering NGO's; 4) support for a variety of statewide master-apprentice and educational programs aimed at passing along traditional artistic knowledge and skills; and 5) federal recognition of master traditional artists.

Each of these strategies is programmatic, rather than prescriptive, and is guided by peer panel recommendations rather than administrative directive. The major portion of our agency's investment is in the funding of *public presentation of folk artists and their work.* One of the most successful areas of funding has been the support of free community-wide festivals that feature music, dance, craft, storytelling, and foodways of the region. Frequently these festivals also present nationally-known traditional artists who might have a connection to the traditions of a particular locale. The most important factor contributing to the impact of these festivals, however, is the level of cultural expertise applied to the selection and presentation of the featured artists. In Butte, Montana, a town of 30,000 people, an annual festival attracts over 165,000 attendees and has an estimated local economic impact of over 15 million dollars. Beyond the crowds and the influx of cash, the festival each year becomes a temporary cultural commons where Native Americans and cowboys, recent immigrants and old settlers, share a civic space and experience a diverse array of expressive traditions.

Other public activities such as exhibitions, touring programs, and media presentations have the same intent – to foreground folk and traditional artists for the public by shining a spotlight on their work and amplifying their artistic voices. Increasingly, new technologies using webcasts and digital presentations through social media are significant components our applications.

Funding for *fieldwork and documentation*, in much the same manner as the inventories described in the UNESCO Intangible Cultural Heritage Convention, allows the identification and documentation of the varied cultural traditions within the country. This is especially important in identifying new communities, new artistic traditions, and emergent forms of artistic expression. In the early years of our funding, more expansive statewide surveys were common, often leading to an exhibition of a particular state's artistic material. More recently, with new immigrant groups and increasingly dispersed and mobile populations, targeted surveys looking at specific cultural groups or underserved areas of the state are more the norm. Surveys over the past few years have included documentation: of polka music in a Midwestern state, of crafts along the Arizona-Mexican border; of dance traditions of Bolivian immigrants living in the suburbs of Washington, DC; of foodways of selected counties in the state of Texas; and of local palm-leaf hat-making traditions in Hawaii.

Funding for *master-apprentice and educational programs* has been one of the most effective ways to address endangered cultural knowledge and artistic skills. Currently there are 35 ongoing statewide apprenticeship programs supported across the United States, pairing master artists with apprentices in intensive one-on-one training. The state of Missouri recently celebrated its 25th year of supporting, with NEA assistance, folk arts apprenticeships. Over that period, 343 apprenticeships have been funded serving over 500 artists working in music, craft, dance and oral traditions. The Maine Indian Basketmakers have been supported for over 15 years to administer a master-apprentice program in basketmaking. They report that when they started the program there were fewer than a dozen basketmakers under 50 in the four Maine tribes who made baskets. The average age of the 60 founding members was 63. Today there are over 200 basketmakers with an average age of 40. These intensive training programs have proven to be an especially effective way of passing along cultural knowledge beyond the artistic skills involved, including serving as a means to encourage the use of endangered tribal languages. Today we see cases of former apprentices now serving as masters in apprenticeship programs.

Key to the success of the above programs has been the establishment and maintenance of a *network of folk arts specialists at state, regional, and*

local arts agencies, as well as cooperating non-profit organizations (NGO's).
From the earliest days of a folk arts funding program at the NEA, it was
realized that the folk arts often operate under the radar screen in informal settings without the benefit of institutional or economic support. One
could say that these artistic traditions exist in the realm of both the intangible and the unincorporated. As a result, the development of a strong
infrastructure of cultural expertise in all areas of the U.S. has been a prior-
ity, in order to provide an adaptable and responsive link with individual
artists and cultural communities. State and regional folk arts coordinators serve as eyes and ears in identifying, documenting, and assessing the
needs of folk artists; and these cultural specialists, in turn, provide the
backbone and muscle to carry out programs in collaboration with cultural
communities. Today there are statewide folk arts programs in 44 of the
56 states and special jurisdictions, offering a variety of services, including
funding opportunities, fieldwork, programmatic activities, apprenticeship
programs, educational initiatives, and technical assistance.

Finally, one of the most successful strategies developed by the Folk &
Traditional Arts discipline at the NEA came with the initiation of the National Heritage Fellowship (http://arts.gov/honors/heritage) program in
1982. This program, the highest form of federal *recognition of folk and traditional artists*, honors master artists for their contributions to our nation's
cultural heritage. The award comes with a fellowship stipend of $25,000
and culminates with a ceremony, banquet, and concert in our nation's
Capital. Over the course of 32 years, 386 awards have been given, recognizing 208 culturally distinct artistic traditions from Apache basketmaking
to Yiddish singing; The awards represent 53 broad genres of expression,
from bonsai to weaving; they include musical performances on 46 different
instruments, and artists maintaining 20 distinct dance traditions.

Bess Lomax Hawes, the former Director of Folk Arts who initiated the
Heritage program eloquently summed up its impact in this way:

> Of all the activities assisted by the Folk Arts Program, these
> fellowships are among the most appreciated and applauded,
> perhaps because they present to Americans a vision of them-
> selves and of their country, a vision somewhat idealized but
> profoundly longed for and so, in significant ways, profoundly
> true. It is a vision of a confident and open-hearted nation,
> where differences can be seen as exciting instead of fear-laden,
> where men of good will, across all manner of racial, linguis-
> tic, and historical barriers, can find common ground in under-
> standing solid craftsmanship, virtuoso techniques, and deeply
> felt experiences.

The success of these five strategies has been dependent upon providing artists and cultural communities with opportunities to imagine their own ways of safeguarding their intangible cultural heritage and then supporting them, however modestly, in that endeavor. Scholars such as Laurijane Smith have pointed out that all heritage is intangible – it is a socially constructed process of meaning-making. Recently my home state of Maryland honored a master artist who was both a carver of duck decoys used for hunting and a taxidermist who mounted the skins and feathers of birds in lifelike poses. One effort results in the creation of a realistic image of a duck carved out of wood while the other produces a life-like re-creation of what had once been a living duck. Each of these endeavors requires a number of intangibles – local knowledge about the natural world, aesthetic choices in imagining the final product, and hard-earned manual skills in executing the piece. When asked about the differences between the two efforts, he said this: "They are very similar. With a wooden decoy you work from the outside in, and in taxidermy you work from the inside out."

It seems to me that our strategies in working with intangible cultural heritage would greatly benefit from this same approach. We need to work both from the inside out and from the outside in. A successful program will depend upon our ability to connect in a deep way with carriers of intangible cultural heritage while at the same time reaching out to our broader citizenry to encourage an appreciation of the value of the diverse cultural assets of our respective nations.

In conclusion, in international forums I always like to point out that the United States is a relatively young nation, by most standards a work in progress, if you will. Our intangible cultural heritage is evolving, mobile, geographically dispersed, and aesthetically diverse. Our work with intangible cultural heritage is also a work in progress but our strategies are consistent with the goals of the UNESCO Convention on the Safeguarding of Intangible Cultural Heritage. The fieldwork and documentation that we support is consistent with the inventory processes described in the convention. The apprenticeships and educational projects in our portfolio address the endangered cultural traditions and also raise public awareness of the value of intangible cultural heritage. The development and maintenance of an infrastructure of cultural expertise is consistent with fostering and strengthening institutions tasked with safeguarding cultural heritage. Funding for public programs and our National Heritage Fellowships contribute significantly to raising public awareness of intangible cultural heritage. A listing of the National Heritage Fellows provides a representative ledger of significant living cultural traditions in the United States.

Boat builder and National Heritage Fellow Ralph Stanley said the process of building a boat is never complete – the builder must continually adjust to new technologies, new design requirements, and new navigational circumstances. He described his work as "like climbing a still-growing tree where you never get to the top." Our work with intangible cultural heritage is similar, it is evolving with these underlying principles: recognition of and respect for the importance of our nation's diverse cultural heritage; understanding that cultural work is an ongoing collaborative process that is best served by listening to the voices of the community; developing multi-faceted and multi-layered programs characterized by both flexibility and continuity; and consistent and persistent commitment of financial resources and human effort to the process. These approaches to cultural conservation and cultural conversation are based on the assumption that signing a convention, achieving inscription on a list, or doing an inventory is a starting point, not the end point of the venture. We will continue to climb that still-growing tree.

Barry Bergey: Letter to Jane Beck

The Graduate School and Office of Research

UNIVERSITY OF MISSOURI-COLUMBIA

Missouri Cultural Heritage Center
400 Hitt Street
Columbia, Missouri 65211
Telephone (314) 882-6296

August 29, 1984

Jane Beck
Vermont Council on the Arts
136 State Street
Montpelier, Vermont 05602

Dear Jane:

Thank you so much for the kind words about the materials
and our program in Missouri. Feel free to quote any
part of the report if you wish. Today it's 106 degrees
and it's just mid-afternoon, so I've had trouble concen-
trating on writing anything about our program. A little
bit of musing on Missouri did produce the following, but
don't feel that you have to use it. Just blame it on
one overheated Missourian if you like.

Working in public sector folk arts activity in Missouri,
I've begun to realize a strong personal identification
with our much maligned yet much beloved state animal--
the mule. The mule is the animal that "God never meant
to exist." Born of two species, the jackass (equus asinus)
and the mare (equus caballus), the mule has had to struggle
for every bit of respect that it's gotten. The folklorist,
a product of academis anthropologus and academis literatus
has often suffered the same fate. Some religious sects
won't work with mules because they're unnatural animals.
I've encountered public sector institutions that feel
the same way about me.

Yet in my more optimistic moments, I realize the positive
qualities of our equine soulmates. Hard work and unequalled
tenacity have won for mules the respect of most grassroots
Missouri citizens. Most consoling of all remains the
realization that the mule is unique to the world in one
very special way--you can kill every one of them and they
still aren't extinct. "Take heart," I tell myself, "both
mules and folklorists most assuredly have a few jackasses
somewhere in their lineage, but with the help of God, or
skilled breeders, or endowments, we shall not merely endure
but prevail!"

Sincerely,

Barry

Barry Bergey
Special Projects Coordinator

BB/pl

In Memoriam: Clyde Faries

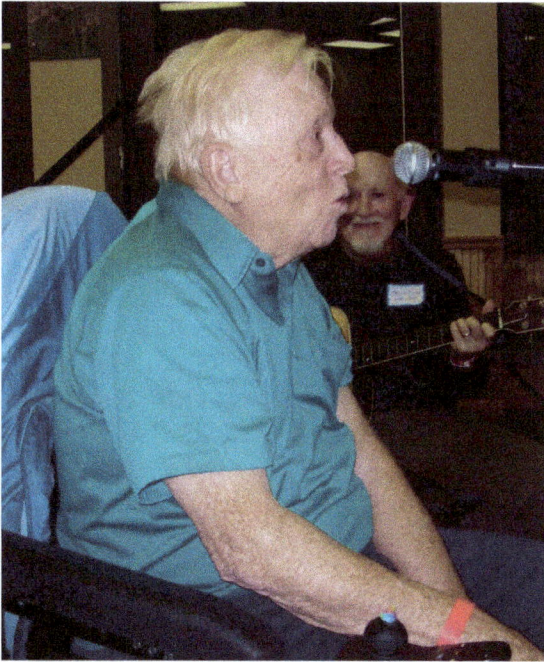

It has been a hard year for the Society, losing some of our longest-serving, most valued members. Among them is Clyde Faries.

Clyde Faries, 90, of Terre du Lac, MO, passed away March 26, 2019 at home surrounded by his loved ones. He was born July 8, 1928, in Rombauer, MO, to the late Darcy Orton and Inis (McIntosh) Faries. He was a member of Trinity Lutheran Church in Park Hills, MO.

Clyde received his PhD in Rhetoric and Public Address from the University of Missouri, and retired as a professor and Chair of the Department of Communication at Western Illinois University. He served terms as President of the Georgia Speech Association and the Illinois Speech and Theatre Association. Retirement allowed him to spend 1990 and 1994 in Changsha, Hunan, China, teaching at the National University of Defense Technology.

With his wife, Liz, Clyde served as president of the Missouri Folklore Society in Sikeston in 1999. He was of enormous assistance to her just three years later when she, Ellen Massey, and Sharon Brock co-chaired the meeting at Trout Lodge in Potosi.

His life outside the classroom included writing and directing "Mystery" plays for Elderhostels, playing British and American folk music, pickle ball, and golf. He participated in historical reenactments as well; for example in 2002 he portrayed Farmington's Sheriff Thomas McMullin, who served from 1860 until his death in 1880. Like Clyde, McMullin played the harmonica beautifully.

Sometime before 2000, Clyde produced *A Bunch of Thyme: 22 Heritage Songs* as a cassette. In 2004, he produced *The Fields of Athenry* CD as a tribute to Donald Lance and Ruth Barton. The CD was well received in Athenry itself a few years ago. It continues to be a popular MFS fundraiser, thanks to artists who participated–such as Judy Domeny Bowen, Kathy Fullmer, Jim Hickam, Knox McCrory, Dave and Cathy Para, the Shade Tree Folk Company, and Clyde himself.

A stroke in 2006 left Clyde less physically independent than before, though no less kindly and full of humor. In 2013 he published a memoir, *Yes, Missouri, There Really Is a Bootheel: Growing Up in the Bootheel.* In typical Clyde fashion, he calls it "Life Between the Levees." He summarizes the book, and his heritage, thus:

> I grew up in a frontier society, along with those who, like my
> father, had come from neighboring states to try to make a new
> life in this land of black gumbo and sandy loam, bordered by
> the St. Francis and Mississippi Rivers. They came to tame the
> land and make it their own, and took pride in facing the worst
> that nature could throw at them. I have written this book to let
> others know of the struggles, sorrows, and joys shared by day
> laborers and sharecroppers during the twenties and thirties in
> the Missouri Bootheel that I remember and still love.

Clyde was an adoring husband to his wife Liz (Thomas) Faries and an adoring father to his delightful children, Dixie, Dee, David, and Doug.

He was preceded in death by his parents; brothers, Fred and Highlee Faries; sister, Marie Horton; and half-brothers, George and Joe Richards. He is survived by his wife Elizabeth Marie (Thomas) Faries and by his children: Dixie Perez and husband Efrain, Dee J. (Tom Dahl) Faries, David O.

Faries and wife Carol, Doug Faries and wife Karen; grandchildren, Jason (Sara) Self, Nicole (Gunthar) Weaver, Erin (Chris) Boggs, Becky (Brad) Tipton, Evan (Kiera) Faries, Caleb Faries, James Faries, and Joe Faries; twelve great-grandchildren, and three great-great-grandchildren; sister, Helen Myracle; numerous nieces and nephews, other family members and friends.

Visitation was held at C.Z. Boyer and Son Funeral Home in Desloge, MO, Saturday, March 30, 2019. The service as held at Trinity Lutheran Church in Park Hills, MO, the next day, with Pastor Jarold Rux officiating. Interment was at Hillview Memorial Gardens in Farmington, MO. Memorials were directed to Missouri Folklore Society and to the YMCA at Trout Lodge.

In both Prologue and Epilogue to *Yes, Missouri, There Really Is a Bootheel*, Clyde says he plans to live until he's 120. We wish he'd made it.

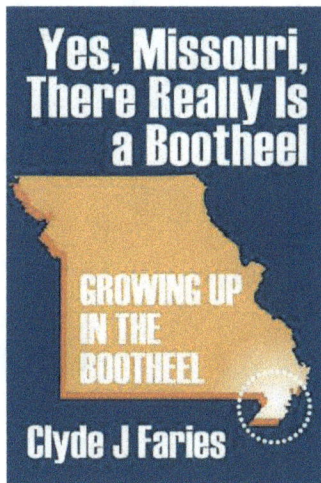

Notes on Contributors

Marti L. Allen is director of the Arkansas State University Museum. She holds a doctorate in classical art and archaeology and a certificate in museum practices from The University of Michigan (1985/86). She has over forty years of experience working in university museums (Arkansas State University Museum, 2006–present; Museum of Peoples and Cultures at Brigham Young University, 1991–2006; Kelsey Museum of Archaeology at University of Michigan-Ann Arbor, 1976–1991).

Barry Bergey is the folklorist we especially honor in this issue of the *Journal*. See pp. 1-2 for a more detailed biography.

Betsy H. Bradley is experienced as a heritage preservation specialist, historian, and professor of history and historic preservation. Her professional and academic interests center on the critique of policy, practice, and the evolving nature of the preservation field. She serves as Academic Specialist for the Goucher Historic Preservation Program, and keenly monitors the ever-changing historic preservation field in the United States. Dr. Bradley has taught in the Goucher Historic Preservation program since 2007. Her courses include Introduction to Historic Preservation, Documentation, and Preservation Public Policy, and she has directed over twenty thesis projects. She has also taught historic preservation at the University of St. Thomas Art History graduate program; Ursuline College's undergraduate program, and in the Youngstown State University's undergraduate and graduate departments. Author of *The Works: The Industrial Architecture of the United States* (Oxford University Press, 1999), she has also written about how property owners addressed old dwellings prior to the creation of formal historic preservation programs. (See *Re-Creating the American Past: Essays on the Colonial Revival*, University of Virginia Press, 2006). Dr. Bradley has over twenty years of experience working with preservation policies and practices—with the New York City Landmarks Preservation Commission and with the commissions of Shaker Heights, Ohio; Taylors Falls, Minnesota; and Spokane, Washington, where she now resides. From 2011 to 2016, she directed the historic preservation program in the City of St. Louis, Missouri. She oversaw the review of thousands of building permits. She has addressed current topics—such as demolition review in a Legacy City; the design of new construction; the regulation of solar panels in historic districts; the integration of historic districts; and form-based zoning. Bradley has a Master's Degree in Historic Preservation from Columbia University and a Ph.D. in History from Case Western Reserve University.

Nancy Chikaraishi AIA is Professor of Architecture at the Hammons School of Architecture at Drury University in Springfield, Missouri. Prior to teaching she practiced architecture in Milwaukee and Chicago. She has led multiple study abroad trips, taking students to Europe and Japan; she often works collaboratively with interdisciplinary experts and with her students. She co-led three design/build projects with students in Joplin, MO after the 2011 tornado and competed in the Solar Decathlon in 2015, taking a solar-powered, tornado-resistant home to Irvine, CA. Her drawings exploring her parent's experiences in the Rohwer Relocation Center were exhibited at the Japanese American Internment Museum in McGehee AR; this heritage was further incorporated into the CORE Performance Company's dance-drama, *Gaman*, for which she did the visual arts. The theatrical performance, supplemented by exhibits, lectures, and storytelling, traveled around Arkansas, Missouri, and elsewhere, commemorating the 70th and 75th anniversaries of the closing of the camps. Chikaraishi's latest project investigates what lies buried beneath Table Rock Lake, a 43,000 acre man-made lake created by damming the White River in Arkansas and Missouri for flood control, electricity production and recreation in 1959. Her website is http://www.nancychikaraishi.com/ .

Kirstin Erickson is Associate Professor of Anthropology and Director of Honors Studies in the Fulbright College of Arts and Sciences at the University of Arkansas. Her first book, *Yaqui Homeland and Homeplace: The Everyday Production of Ethnic Identity* (University of Arizona Press, 2008) considers how memory, landscape narratives, and senses of place shape ethnic and gendered identity among members of the Yaqui Tribe in Sonora, Mexico. Her current book project focuses on Hispano communities in northern New Mexico, where she examines cultural production and the negotiation of heritage and belonging. She studies the ways in which vernacular religion, material representations, and arts activism are deployed in discourses about *Nuevomexicano* heritage and cultural memory. She teaches courses such as these at the University of Arkansas: The U.S.-Mexico Borderlands; Religion in Latin America; Museums and Material Culture; Pilgrimage, Heritage, and Tourism; and Performance Theory.

Her articles have been published in various journals, including the *Journal of American Folklore, Western Folklore, Anthropology and Humanism*, and the *Journal of Folklore Research.*

Gregory Hansen is Professor of Folklore and English at Arkansas State University, where he also teaches in the Heritage Studies Doctoral Program. Hansen specializes in the folklife of America's southern states and teaches courses on folklore, fieldwork, ethnography, literature, American Indian verbal art, mythology, and folk music. He has completed public folklore projects for a range of organizations, including the Smithsonian Institution, Danish Immigrant Museum, Florida Folklife Program, and Kentucky Center for the Arts. Research from these projects has been presented in numerous folklife festivals, museum exhibits, educational programs, media productions, and professional development projects for educators. His research and publications center on folklore and education, public folklore, documentary media, and folk performances. Hansen has also produced documentary videos on oral history and folklife, and he has assisted with the production of audio recordings of traditional music. He has recently published *Florida Fiddler: The Life and Times of Richard Seaman* and various book chapters and articles on fiddling, storytelling, folklore and computers, and on the public presentation of cultural heritage.

Ruth Hawkins grew up on a farm north of St. Louis, Missouri. She served as Executive Director of Arkansas Heritage Sites at Arkansas State University for many years, with overall responsibilities for policies and programs at the Southern Tenant Farmers Museum in Tyronza, Lakeport Plantation in Lake Village, the Hemingway-Pfeiffer Museum and Educational Center in Piggott, the Rohwer Japanese American Relocation Center, and the Johnny Cash Boyhood Home Project in Dyess. Ruth also served as Executive Director of Arkansas Delta Byways, a 15-county association that promotes tourism in Eastern Arkansas and along its two national scenic byways: Crowley's Ridge Parkway and the Arkansas Great River Road. She has recently retired as a faculty member in Arkansas State's Heritage Studies Ph.D. program.

Cherisse Jones-Branch is the James and Wanda Lee Vaughn Endowed Professor of History and Director of the ASTATE Digital Press at Arkansas State University. She teaches courses in U.S., Women's, Civil Rights, Rural, and African American History, and in Heritage Studies. Jones-Branch received her Bachelor's and Master's degrees from the College of Charleston, South Carolina, and a doctorate in History from Ohio State. She has been teaching at Arkansas State since 2003. She is the author of numerous articles on women's Civil Rights and rural activism. In 2014, she published

Crossing the Line: Women and Interracial Activism in South Carolina during and after World War II, with the University Press of Florida. She is the co-editor of *Arkansas Women: Their Lives and Times* (2018, University of Georgia Press). She has a second monograph forthcoming, *Better Living By Their Own Bootstraps: Rural Black Women's Activism in Arkansas*, with the University of Arkansas Press.

Daniel Maher is Associate Professor of Anthropology at the University of Arkansas-Fort Smith. His research focus is cultural heritage tourism with a particular emphasis on how nineteenth century history is converted into frontier and pioneer tourist narratives. He is currently working on his second monograph, *Mythic Pioneers of the Tallgrass Prairie: From Wilderness to Wilder and Back*. It will be a complement to his book *Mythic Frontiers: Forgetting, Remembering, and Profiting with Cultural Heritage Tourism* (2016 University Press of Florida).

Jerome McDonough has been on the faculty of the University of Illinois School of Information Sciences since 2005. His research focuses on socio-technical aspects of information systems, with particular concentrations on issues of metadata and description as well as on digital preservation of complex media, and on software. Prior to joining the faculty at the iSchool, Dr. McDonough served as the head of the Digital Library Development Team for New York University. He has also been an active participant in metadata standards activities for digital libraries, having served as chair of the METS Editorial Board, as well as serving on the NISO Standards Development Committee and the ODRL International Advisory Board. Most recently, his research has included heading the Preserving Virtual Worlds initiative and collaborating with researchers at Carnegie Mellon University on the Olive Executable Archive for software preservation. Dr. McDonough completed his doctoral studies at the U.C. Berkeley School of Library & Information Studies in 2000. His dissertation, *Under Construction: The Application of a Feminist Sociology to Information Systems Design*, investigated the construction of identity in graphical, computed-mediated communication systems, and the influence that CMC system designers may have on their users' presentations of self

Amanda Minks is an Associate Professor of Anthropology and Ethnomusicology in the Honors College of the University of Oklahoma. She is the author of the book *Voices of Play: Miskitu Children's Speech and Song on the Atlantic Coast of Nicaragua* (University of Arizona Press, 2013), and she is currently working on a historical book about indigenous music and heritage in the Americas. She was co-director of the NEH-funded project "Community Archiving of Native American Music" from 2016-2018.

Bryan Moore is Professor of English at Arkansas State University and has taught in the Heritage Studies program. He specializes in rhetoric, nineteenth-century American literature, and environmental literature. He is the author of *Ecology and Literature: Ecocentric Personification from Antiquity to the Twenty-first Century* (2008) and *Ecological Literature and the Critique of Anthropocentrism* (2017).

Michelle L. Stefano is a Folklife Specialist (Research and Programs) at the American Folklife Center, Library of Congress. She earned her BA in art history (Brown University, 2000), MA in international museum studies (Gothenburg University, Sweden, 2004) and PhD in heritage studies at the International Centre for Cultural and Heritage Studies at Newcastle University (UK) in 2010. From 2011-2016, Stefano worked for Maryland Traditions, the folklife program of the state of Maryland; she was its Co-Director from 2015-2016. From 2012-2016, she led the partnership between Maryland Traditions and the University of Maryland, Baltimore County, where she was Visiting Assistant Professor in American Studies. She co-edited the 2017 *Routledge Companion to Intangible Cultural Heritage* and *Safeguarding Intangible Cultural Heritage* (Boydell & Brewer, 2012). And she edited the *International Journal of Heritage Studies* 2016 special issue, *Critical Heritage Work: Public Folklore in the U.S* (vol. 22 no. 8).

Gabriel Tait is Assistant Professor of Diversity and Media in the CCIM, Department of Journalism, Ball State Univesity. He is currently serving as the Phi Kappa Phi president-elect for the Ball State University chapter. His research areas include photojournalism, diversity and media, participatory photography, the role photography plays in constructing and representing cultural identities. He is co-editor of *Narratives of Storytelling across Cultures: The Complexities of Intercultural Communication*, Lexington Books— Fall 2019. He also created his visual research methodology called, "Sight Beyond My Sight" (SBMS). Prior to teaching in the university, he served for 20 years as a national and international newspaper photojournalist for the *St. Louis Post-Dispatch* and the *Detroit Free Press*, covering events in Iraq, Kosovo, Egypt, and numerous other countries.

Natalie Underberg-Goode is Associate Professor of Digital Media and Folklore in the University of Central Florida School of Visual Arts and Design, where she is currently serving as Graduate Program Coordinator for the Emerging Media M.F.A.–Digital Media Track, and for the Digital Media M.A. degree. She is also core faculty in the Texts & Technology Ph.D. program. Her research examines the use of digital media to preserve and disseminate folklore and cultural heritage, with a focus on digital storytelling and participatory new media design and practice. She is author (with Elayne Zorn) of the book *Digital Ethnography: Anthropology, Narrative, and New Media* (University of Texas Press, 2013), as well as more than 20 articles, book chapters, and conference proceedings. She has been PI or co-PI on research and teaching grants totaling over $200,000. These include two Florida Humanities Council and two Florida Department of State Division of Cultural Affairs grants. Her research has been presented at 22 national and international conferences, including the Bilan du Film Ethnographique seminar in Paris, France, and the American Folklore Society. In addition to research, Dr. Underberg-Goode has developed core courses for the Digital Media and Latin American Studies programs, and electives for the Film and Texts and Technology programs at UCF. She has taught or teaches courses in a variety of areas including digital storytelling, research methods, video game history and development, digital media production, and Latin American popular culture. She has served her profession through such activities as co-organizing four international and three regional conferences, serving as the incoming chair of the Department of State Bureau of Historic Preservation, Florida Folklife Council. She has mentored students for the Society for Visual Anthropology, and is the book reviews co-editor (U.S. and Canada) for *Visual Anthropology Review*, and the digital stories curator for *The Florida Review*.

Thomas Walker received his academic training in the disciplines of anthropology, history, and folklore, earning his PhD at Indiana University. He is currently the director of the Masters programs in Environmental Studies and Historic Preservation at Goucher College and had previously served as a co-director of the MA in its Cultural Sustainability program. Dividing his time between these two programs, he also promotes their complementarity, interrelationship, and common focus on a human dimensions approach to the study of natural and built environments. He maintains a long-standing interest in material culture, vernacular architecture, cultural geography, preservation, community engagement and sustainability. He has worked in museums and arts organizations involved in historic preservation projects, including a virtual museum developed at Indiana University—based on a collection of historic log buildings and documentation of traditional culture of the area. He has also conducted oral histories of historic preservation in Indiana and documented maritime culture in the Chesapeake Bay region as well as in New York harbor to contextualize the history of the seaport and its collection of historic vessels and buildings. As a venture philanthropist, he has served as a trustee for a foundation — www.walker-foundation.org — which funds research, policy, and projects investigating environmental economics in areas of climate change, energy and tax policy, ecosystem services, ecotourism, and sustainability in forests and fisheries.

Jeremy C. Wells is an assistant professor in the Historic Preservation Program at the University of Maryland, College Park, and a Fulbright scholar. His research explores ways to make built heritage conservation practice more responsive to people through the use of applied social science research methods from environmental psychology, humanistic geography, anthropology, and community development/public health. Wells is chair of the Environmental Design Research Association's (EDRA's) board. At EDRA, he created the Historic Environment Knowledge Network to engage academics and practitioners in addressing the person/place and environment/behavior aspects of heritage conservation. Wells runs the heritagestudies.org web site that explores how to evolve heritage conservation practice using critical heritage studies theory to better balance meanings and power between experts and most stakeholders. He is co-editor of *Human-Centered Built Heritage Conservation: Theory and Evidence-based Practice* (2019, Routledge.

Michael Ann Williams has taught folklore at Western Kentucky University since 1986. In 2004, she became head of the newly created Department of Folk Studies and Anthropology. Her research interests have included social and symbolic use of space in vernacular architecture, government policy and its impact on Appalachian communities, and cultural representation and the staging of tradition. She has worked on applied projects with her graduate students, including an oral history project documenting the former logging town of Ravensford, North Carolina, part of a larger cultural resource documentation effort accompanying a transfer of land from the Great Smoky Mountains National Park to the Eastern Band of Cherokee Indians. She has chaired the Kentucky Historic Preservation Review Board, is an advisor to the Kentucky Oral History Commission, and an active member of the Vernacular Architecture Forum. She is a past president of the American Folklore Society.

www.ingramcontent.com/pod-product-compliance
Lightning Source LLC
Chambersburg PA
CBHW051735020426
42333CB00014B/1323